Stop Faking It!

Finally Understanding Science   So You Can Teach It

MATH

Stop Faking It!

Finally Understanding Science   So You Can Teach It

MATH

NATIONAL SCIENCE TEACHERS ASSOCIATION

Arlington, Virginia

NATIONAL SCIENCE TEACHERS ASSOCIATION

Claire Reinburg, Director
Judy Cusick, Senior Editor
Andrew Cocke, Associate Editor
Betty Smith, Associate Editor
Robin Allan, Book Acquisitions Coordinator

ART AND DESIGN Will Thomas, Director
   Brian Diskin, Illustrator
PRINTING AND PRODUCTION Catherine Lorrain-Hale, Director
   Nguyet Tran, Assistant Production Manager
   Jack Parker, Electronic Prepress Technician

NATIONAL SCIENCE TEACHERS ASSOCIATION
Gerald F. Wheeler, Executive Director
David Beacom, Publisher

08   07   06   4   3   2   1

Library of Congress Cataloging-in-Publication Data
Robertson, William C.
  Math / by William C. Robertson.
     p. cm.—(Stop faking it! finally understanding science so you can teach it)
  Includes index.
  ISBN 0-87355-240-7
  1. Mathematics—Study and teaching—Popular works. I. Title. II. Series: Robertson, William C. Stop
faking it!
  Q11.2.R63 2006
  510.071—dc22
                    2005033676

Contents

Preface

The book you have in your hands is the seventh in the *Stop Faking It!* series. The previous six books have been on various science topics, so obviously a book on math is a slight departure from what I have done so far. The focus on understanding rather than memorization, though, remains. When I speak of understanding, I'm not talking about what rules and formulas to apply when, but rather knowing the meaning behind all the rules, formulas, and procedures. I *know* that it is possible for science and math to make sense at a *deep level*—deep enough that you can teach it to others with confidence and comfort.

Why do science and math have such a bad reputation as being so difficult? What makes them so difficult to understand? Well, my contention is that science and math are *not* difficult to understand. It's just that from kindergarten through graduate school, we present the material *way* too fast and at too abstract a level. To truly understand science and math, you need *time* to wrap your mind around the concepts. However, very little science and math instruction allows that necessary time. Unless you have the knack for understanding abstract ideas in a quick presentation, you can quickly fall behind as the material flies over your head. Unfortunately, the solution many people use to keep from falling behind is to *memorize* the material. Memorizing your way through the material is a surefire way to feel uncomfortable when it comes time to teach the material to others. You have a difficult time answering questions that aren't stated explicitly in the textbook, you feel inadequate, and let's face it—it just isn't any fun!

So, how do you go about *understanding* science and math? You could pick up a high school or college science textbook and do your best to plow through the ideas, but that can get discouraging quickly. You could plunk down a few bucks and take an introductory college course, but you might be smack in the middle of a too-much-material-too-fast situation. Chances are, also, that the undergraduate credit you would earn wouldn't do the tiniest thing to help you on your teaching pay scale. Elementary and middle school textbooks generally include brief explanations of the concepts, but the emphasis is definitely on the word *brief*. Finally, you can pick up one or fifty "resource" books that contain many cool classroom activities but also include too brief, sometimes incorrect, and vocabulary-laden explanations.

There is an established method for helping people learn concepts, and that method is known as the Learning Cycle. Basically, it consists of having someone do a hands-on activity or two, or even just think about various questions or situations, followed by explanations based on those activities. By connecting new concepts to existing ideas, activities, or experiences, people tend to develop understanding rather than memorization. Each chapter in this book, then, is broken up into two kinds of sections.

One kind of section is titled, "Things to do before you read the explanation," and the other is titled, "The explanation." If you actually do the things I ask prior to reading the explanations, I guarantee you'll have a more satisfying experience and a better chance of grasping the material.

I do suggest that you read the section titled "About This Book" before you start plowing through the material.

Dedication

I dedicate this book to the two best math teachers I ever had—Drexel Pope in seventh and eighth grade and Harmon Unkrich in high school.

About the Author

As the author of NSTA Press's *Stop Faking It!* series, Bill Robertson believes science can be both accessible and fun—if it's presented so that people can readily understand it. Robertson is a science education writer, reviews and edits science materials, and frequently conducts inservice teacher workshops as well as seminars at NSTA conventions. He has also taught physics and developed K–12 science curricula, teacher materials, and award-winning science kits. He earned a master's degree in physics from the University of Illinois and a PhD in science education from the University of Colorado.

About the Illustrator

The recently-out-of-debt, soon-to-be-famous, humorous illustrator Brian Diskin grew up outside of Chicago. He graduated from Northern Illinois University with a degree in commercial illustration, after which he taught himself cartooning. His art has appeared in many books, including *The Beerbellie Diet* and *How a Real Locomotive Works*. You can also find his art in newspapers, on greeting cards, on T-shirts, and on refrigerators. At any given time he can be found teaching watercolors and cartooning, and hopefully working on his ever-expanding series of *Stop Faking It!* books. You can view his work at *www.briandiskin.com*.

About This Book

I'm thinking that many of you are sitting back, looking at this book, and wondering why in the world I'm writing it. Sure, it's difficult to understand lots of science concepts, but everyone understands mathematics, right? You add, subtract, multiply, divide, mess around with fractions, solve equations, and all that, and just about everyone who has to teach math knows all the rules. Well yes, just about everyone who teaches math *does* understand the rules, but there's more to math than the rules. Here's one of my favorite examples:

When you add two fractions, you have to get a common denominator. Then in order to add these fractions, you add the numerators of the fractions but don't add the denominators. The denominator of the result is the same as the denominator of the two fractions you're adding. When you multiply two fractions together, however, you don't need to get a common denominator. You simply multiply the numerators together, and then you multiply the denominators together.

Yep, those are the rules for adding and multiplying fractions. Now. . .do those rules make sense? Why do you need a common denominator when adding fractions, but not when multiplying them? Why is it that when adding fractions you add the numerators but not the denominators, yet when multiplying fractions you multiply both the numerators and the denominators?

If the questions above bother you a bit, or if you have never even thought about them, then perhaps this book is for you. There are great reasons behind the rules for adding and multiplying fractions, just as there are great reasons for just about everything you do in math. Many people learn math, however, without ever learning the reasoning behind the rules.

So what's wrong with just knowing the rules? Well, without understanding the reasoning behind the rules of math, chances are you are simply memorizing procedures. If you're memorizing procedures, then chances are you are teaching your students to memorize procedures. There's a big difference between memorizing math and really understanding it. In my humble opinion, when you really understand what's going on in math (or science, or anything else), then you are more comfortable teaching it and might just do a better job of teaching it.

Which brings us to the next point—the broad scope of this book. I begin with adding numbers in Base 10, and end up with calculus. Why does a kindergarten or second grade teacher need to know how to solve algebraic equations, figure out geometric formulas, and be able to do calculus? The short answer is that you don't need to know how to *do* these math calculations, but that you just might benefit from *understanding* these math calculations. When you know more than your students are likely to ask about, you feel more comfortable. On the occasion that your students *do* ask complicated questions, wouldn't it be nice to at least have a basic understanding from which to answer the questions? Answer: yes.

Which brings us to another point. The purpose of this book is to help you gain a deep understanding of the meaning behind the rules and operations of math. The purpose is *not* to ensure that you will be able to *do* the various calculations with proficiency. You won't become an expert at solving algebraic equations, solving geometry problems, or solving calculus problems by going through this book. To become proficient, you need more than understanding; you need lots and lots of practice. Any math course or textbook in the appropriate subject area can guide you through that practice. What I'm trying to do is make that process less painful, should you decide to pursue it.

And another point. Because this math book is part of a science book series, I will usually take the scientist's point of view rather than the mathematician's point of view whenever there is a conflict. As a rule, scientists tend to be just a wee bit less formal in their use of math than are mathematicians. Makes sense, because for the most part math is a tool for scientists. Scientists bend the strict rules of math when it makes sense to do so. For example, division by zero is absolutely undefined in the rules of math, but scientists tend to think in terms of dividing by things so close to zero that those things are essentially equal to zero. So, when they see division by zero, they don't always think that's a terrible thing. That said, many scientific theories have grown from pure mathematics. I don't want to give the impression that math is somehow secondary to science; it isn't. It's just that scientists and mathematicians sometimes view math differently.

I hope that whatever level of science or math you teach, you find this book useful. If some of the early chapters are second nature to you, by all means ignore them. If some of the later chapters seem like something you'll never use, by all means put them away and maybe revisit them at another time. All I'm trying to do is provide a perspective on math that, all too often, doesn't find its way to our students.

Finally, as you go through this book, you will notice a number of text boxes that are labeled *Guidepost*. My most valuable reviewer, my wife, complained that as she went through the text she sometimes got lost as to the purpose of a given section. To make things clearer, I added these Guideposts. They are there to remind you of the purpose of an activity or what exactly I'm explaining at a given point. Think of them as a tool for helping you stay on the same road I'm traveling.

What's Behind the Rules?

I'm going to begin this book with what might seem to you to be math that's so basic it's trivial. We're going to start with addition, subtraction, multiplication, division, fractions, and a few other things. So, your first thought might be, "I learned this by second grade—what's to understand?" Well, maybe you do have a solid understanding of these topics. If so, just breeze on through this chapter. Before you do that, though, realize that in this chapter I will be demonstrating the basic difference between memorizing rules and really understanding the process. Therefore, you might want to read this chapter for that reason alone. As I try to demonstrate this difference, know that I am fully aware of the many excellent math resources that do teach understanding, at least in the early grades. For those of you teaching grades K–2, many of the hands-on activities designed to help with understanding in this book will look familiar.

"Folks, it doesn't have to be like this!"

Things to do before you read the explanation

Gather together about 35 blocks, marbles, peanuts, pinecones, small plastic counting bears, rocks, pennies, or just about any other item that you can count easily. For simplicity, I'll assume from here on out that you have blocks. Make a group of 13 blocks and a separate group of 19 blocks. Then push the blocks together in one large group and count them (I told you this was basic! Bear with me). See Figure 1.1.

Figure 1.1

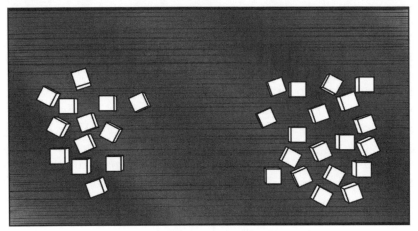

One group of 13 and one group of 19

Both groups combined

Okay, now return the blocks to their original groups of 13 and 19, with the following rule. Whenever you have a group of blocks that is larger than 10, you have to create separate stacks of 10 and a final group of what's left over. So now your groups of blocks should look like Figure 1.2.

Figure 1.2

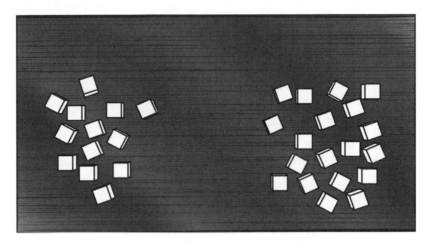

One group of 13 and one group of 19

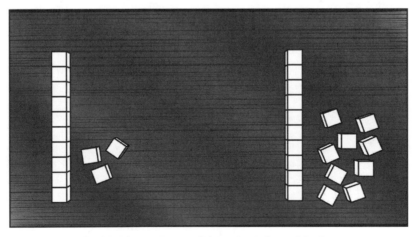

Divided into groups of Tens plus leftover blocks

Next combine all those blocks, still following the above rule for grouping in tens. You should get something like Figure 1.3. Yes, this does look like the drawings in the math workbooks you used back in first grade.

Figure 1.3

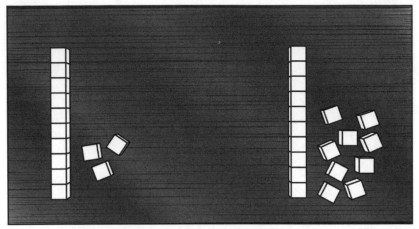

Each group still divided into groups of Tens

Both groups combined and divided into groups of Tens

The explanation

No big surprise that what we're doing here is adding things. The simplest way to add is to put two separate groups of things together and count them. It's more complicated to separate the items into groups of 10 and groups of less-than-10, but we have a shorthand way of doing that. We represent the number of items in a group with **place value** numbers, as in 13 and 19. The number 13 means we have one group of 10 and one group of 3 and the number 19 means we have one group of 10 and one group of 9. That representation uses what we call the **Base 10** number system. In that system, the numbers you write represent how much of each place value you have. Figure 1.4 shows the place values in the Base 10 system, along with the representations for the numbers 13 and 19.

Figure 1.4

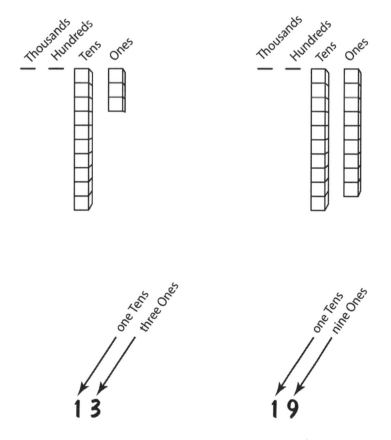

Guidepost The Base 10 counting system and why you "carry" numbers when adding.

We also have a shorthand way of adding these numbers. We write the numbers above each other. Then we add the groups of single items, represented by the numbers 3 and 9 in our example. That gives us more than 10, so we add an extra 1 in the tens place and put what's left over in our final group of ones. It looks like Figure 1.5

Figure 1.5

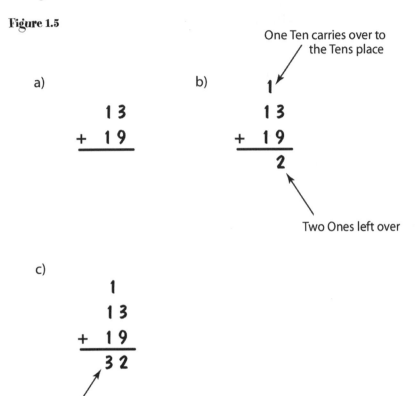

a)

$$
\begin{array}{r}
1\,3 \\
+\ 1\,9 \\
\hline
\end{array}
$$

b)

One Ten carries over to the Tens place

$$
\begin{array}{r}
1 \\
1\,3 \\
+\ 1\,9 \\
\hline
2
\end{array}
$$

Two Ones left over

c)

$$
\begin{array}{r}
1 \\
1\,3 \\
+\ 1\,9 \\
\hline
3\,2
\end{array}
$$

We end up with three Tens

Simple. So what's the point? Why am I spending time on adding two numbers? To illustrate how we often move too quickly to the math shorthand notation and forget about the underlying process. Ask any sixth grader to add 13 and 19, and he or she will have little trouble. The next time you do this, however, you might ask that sixth grader why he or she "carried the one" when adding. Chances are, not all sixth graders will know why they did that. In fact, average adults might not know why that's the thing to do—it's just the thing to do. So, even though we teach addition in early grades by explicitly showing what place value is and why we group things in tens, hundreds, and thousands when adding in Base 10, people have a tendency to forget the process when doing simple addition. This illustrates the difference between simply following math rules and knowing the reasoning behind the math rules. You can "carry the 1" because it's the right thing to do, or you can do that procedure *plus* know why it's the correct procedure. Before moving on, make sure you understand why it is sometimes appropriate to "carry" a 1 over to a different column when adding. Also make sure you understand that the 1 you carry can represent one ten, one hundred, one thousand, and so on.

More things to do before you read more explanation*

We're going to combine blocks again, using new rules for grouping the blocks. Here's the first new rule. Whenever you have 25 or more blocks, you must put them together first in groups of 25. If you have fewer than 25 blocks, then start putting them in groups of 5 until you have fewer than 5 blocks left. Apply this rule to your separate collections of 13 and 19 blocks, and then apply it to the combined group of 32 blocks. This should look like Figures 1.6a and 1.6b.

Figure 1.6a

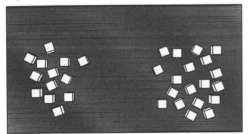

Original groups of 13 and 19

Figure 1.6b

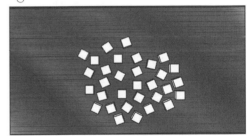

Our group of 32 blocks

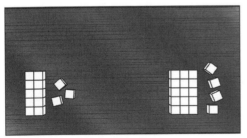

Groups of 13 and 19 divided into groups of Fives

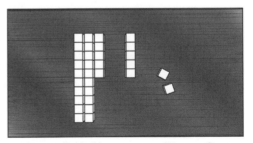

Group divided into groups of Twenty-fives, Fives, and leftovers

---

* The purpose of this section and the next section is to help you gain a better understanding of place value and how it applies to basic math operations. Although using bases other than Base 10 used to be common in elementary and middle school math curricula, it is seldom used these days. So, if these two sections help you understand, great. If they confuse you, feel free to move on without fear that you will be severely handicapped in your reading of the rest of this book or in your teaching.

Time to redo things with a different rule. Whenever you have 32 or more blocks, you must first put them together in groups of 32. If you have fewer than 32 blocks, begin putting them together in groups of 16. If you have fewer than 16 blocks, begin putting them together in groups of 8. If you have fewer than 8 blocks, next put them together in groups of 4. Finally, put what's left into groups of 2, until you have either no blocks left or 1 block left. Figures 1.7a and 1.7b show what you should end up with.

Figure 1.7a

Original groups of 13 and 19 blocks

Figure 1.7b

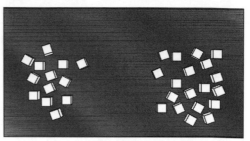

Original groups of 13 and 19 blocks

Groups separated into groups of Sixteens, Eights, Fours, and Twos

Groups combined into groups of Thirty-twos

More explanation

What you just did in the previous section is group things according to bases other than Base 10. You first used Base 5 and then used Base 2. Of course, you might not have realized that you were using these other bases, which is why I'm writing this explanation section. The mere mention of a base other than Base 10 will cause most people to cringe. The process is really the same, though. The place values in **Base 5** are as shown in Figure 1.8.

Figure 1.8

One Hundred Twenty-Fives   Twenty-Fives   Fives   Ones

—　—　—　—

Using Base 5, the number 13 is written as 23_5, meaning there are two groups of five and three ones left over.* If that confuses you a bit, look back at Figure 1.6 and ahead to Figure 1.9. The number 23_5 merely represents the groups you created for your collection of 13 blocks. Similarly, the number 19 is written as 34_5, meaning there are three groups of five and four ones left over.

Figure 1.9

a) The number 13 written in Base 5

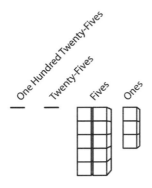 

b) The number 19 written in Base 5

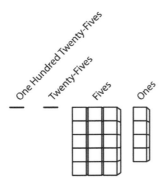 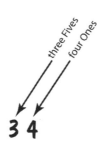

> **Guidepost** Applying the operations in the Base 10 system to the Base 5 system in order to help with understanding the Base 10 system.

---

*Note the subscript 5 on the number 23 is there to make it clear that we're using a base other than Base 10. If there isn't a subscript on a number, you can assume the number is Base 10. If there is a subscript, then the subscript indicates the base being used. Don't worry, though. You'll only have to worry about different bases for this section.

When adding the numbers 23_5 and 34_5, the shorthand notation looks like Figure 1.10.

Figure 1.10

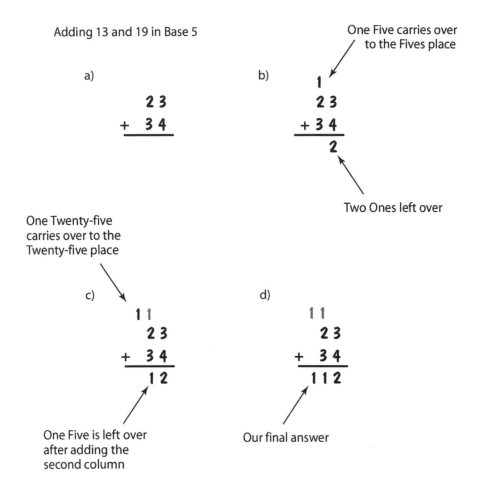

Adding 13 and 19 in Base 5

a)
```
    2 3
+   3 4
_____
```

b)

One Five carries over to the Fives place
```
  1
  2 3
+ 3 4
_____
    2
```
Two Ones left over

c)

One Twenty-five carries over to the Twenty-five place
```
  1 1
    2 3
+   3 4
_____
    1 2
```
One Five is left over after adding the second column

d)
```
  1 1
    2 3
+   3 4
_____
  1 1 2
```
Our final answer

Now we're going to move on to **Base 2**, also known as the **binary number system**. The Base 2 place values are shown in Figure 1.11.

Figure 1.11

a) The number 13 written in Base 2

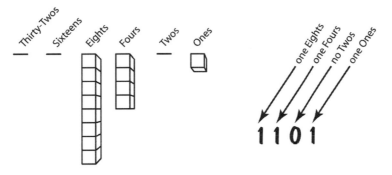

b) The number 19 written in Base 2

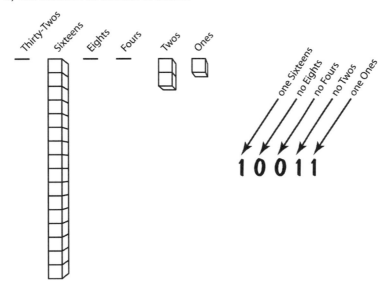

Guidepost Applying the operations in the Base 10 system to the Base 2 system in order to help with understanding the Base 10 system.

We write the number 13 in Base 2 as 1101_2, because there is one eight, one four, zero twos, and one one. The number 19 in Base 2 is 10011_2, because there is one sixteen, zero eights, zero fours, one two, and one one. Check that these numbers correspond to the groups you created in Figure 1.7. The groups of blocks you get when you combine everything together in Figure 1.7 are a physical representation of the Base 2 number 100000_2, because you simply have one group with 32 blocks in it. We can add binary numbers using shorthand, just as with Base 5 and Base 10. Figure 1.12 shows this.

Figure 1.12

Adding 13 and 19 in Base 2

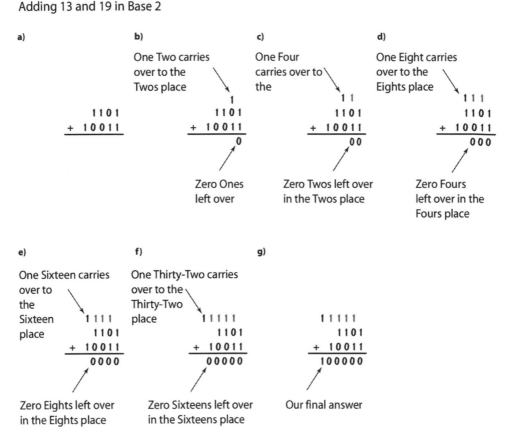

Base 5 and Base 2 place values are not second nature to most of us, which is why it takes a bit of thought to use the shorthand method. My point in discussing different bases is to illustrate the "reasoning behind the rule" when you add in Base 10.

Even more things to do before reading even more explanations

Time to subtract instead of add. Get more blocks (or pennies, or whatever) until you have 43 of them. Group them according to Base 10 place values, meaning you need four stacks of 10 blocks for the tens place and 3 blocks left over for the ones place. What you are going to do is subtract, or take away, 16 blocks from these groups. The catch, though, is that you can't just take away 16 blocks. You have to keep track of the place values, meaning you have to take 6 blocks away from the blocks in the ones group and one group of 10 blocks away from the tens group. See Figure 1.13.

Can't do it, can you?

Figure 1.13

The number 43

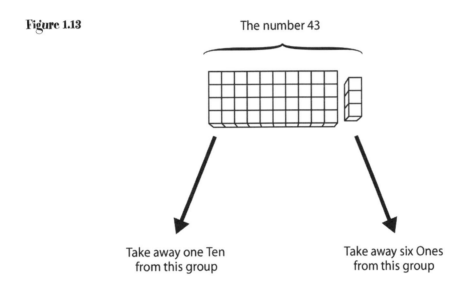

Take away one Ten
from this group

Take away six Ones
from this group

Even more explanation

You can't subtract 16 from 43 in the way I asked you to, because you hit a snag when you try to subtract 6 ones from only 3 ones. There's a solution to this problem. You simply "borrow" one stack of tens from the tens group and place it in the ones group. Now you have 13 ones, and it's easy to subtract 6 ones from this group. Having sent one stack of 10 to the ones group, you now have three groups of 10 left in the tens column. Subtracting one 10 (from the 16) from this group leaves two tens. Two tens and seven ones gives you the number 27. All of this is in Figure 1.14. Figure 1.15 shows this process using shorthand notation for subtraction.

Figure 1.14

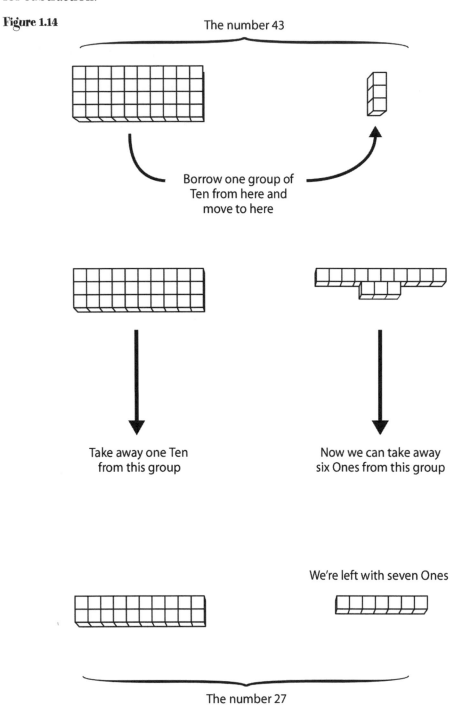

The number 43

Borrow one group of Ten from here and move to here

Take away one Ten from this group

Now we can take away six Ones from this group

We're left with seven Ones

The number 27

Figure 1.15

Subtraction in Base 10

a)

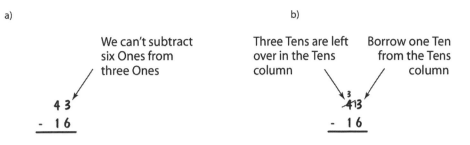

We can't subtract
six Ones from
three Ones

4 3
- 1 6

b)

Three Tens are left
over in the Tens
column

Borrow one Ten
from the Tens
column

4̸13

- 1 6

c)

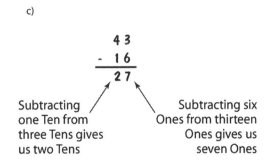

4 3
- 1 6
  2 7

Subtracting
one Ten from
three Tens gives
us two Tens

Subtracting six
Ones from thirteen
Ones gives us
seven Ones

Guidepost Addressing subtraction in Base 10, and why you "borrow."

More things to do before you read more explanation

More fun with blocks (or whatever you're using), and simple fun at that. Make 6 groups of 5 blocks each. How many blocks do you have altogether? Now make a big group of 33 blocks. Begin separating these blocks into groups of 5. How many groups of 5 blocks do you end up with? How many blocks are left over? Yep, easy.

Next take a group of 4 blocks and separate it into 4 groups. How many blocks in each group? Try separating a group of 8 blocks into 8 equal groups. How many in each group? Suppose you separated 356 blocks into 356 groups. Take a wild guess at how many blocks would be in each group.

More explanation

Probably not a big surprise to you that you just multiplied and divided using your blocks. Six groups of 5 blocks each add up to 30 blocks. That's the same as saying that

6 · 5 = 30.* This points out that multiplication is nothing more than repeated addition. 6 · 5 is the same as 5 + 5 + 5 + 5 + 5 + 5. Also, 7 · 99 means add up 99 seven times. This might not be a great revelation to you, but I'm keeping with the idea of stressing understanding the meaning behind operations. I'm sure you can find people who know their multiplication tables but would be baffled by the question, *"Why* does 4 · 7 equal 28?" The answer is easy if you interpret 4 · 7 as 7 + 7 + 7 + 7. The blocks also make it obvious why multiplying a number by the number 1 just gives you the original number. One pile of 5 blocks results in a total of 5 blocks, so 1 · 5 = 5. Similarly, 1 · 456 = 456.

> **Guidepost** Using physical analogies to explain multiplication and division.

The next thing I had you do was separate a group of 33 blocks into groups of five. You should have ended up with 6 groups of 5, with 3 blocks left over, as in Figure 1.16.

Figure 1.16

33 blocks

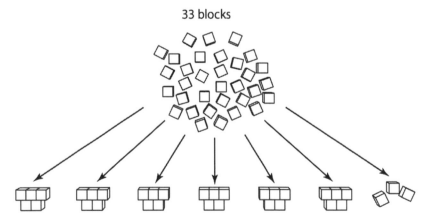

Six groups of 5 blocks with 3 left over

---

* For most of this book, I'll be using a dot (·) to represent multiplication. There's a reason for that. If I use the traditional x for multiplication, then we'll run into trouble when we start using variables in later chapters. I'll reserve x for the *letter* x.

This is just the process of **division**. By separating the collection of 33 into groups of 5, you are *dividing* 33 by 5. In this sense, division is the reverse of multiplication, and can be thought of as repeated subtraction. In dividing 33 by 5, you successively subtract groups of 5 until you can no longer do so. The number of groups of 5 you end up with, plus the leftover blocks, is the answer to 33 ÷ 5. The 3 blocks left over are called the **remainder**, but you already knew that. In math notation, we simply say 33 ÷ 5 = 6 R 3. Yes, I know you're more sophisticated than that, and can express the remainder as a fraction or a decimal—I'll get to that in the next chapter.

Finally, let's talk about dividing a collection of 4 blocks into 4 separate groups, dividing a collection of 8 blocks into 8 groups, and so on. You always end up with one block in each group. All that means is that when you divide a number by itself you always get the answer of 1. Seems trivial, but it's quite an important concept for later material. Anything divided by itself equals 1. Think about blocks so it isn't some kind of memorized rule of math. It makes sense. Of course, we can also use symbols to express this, as in 6 ÷ 6 = 1, 4 ÷ 4 = 1, and 156 ÷ 156 = 1.

And even more things to do before you read even more explanation

> **Guidepost** Using blocks to see what happens when you change the order of numbers in addition.

In this section, you're going to use blocks to model the process of altering order and grouping when using addition, multiplication, subtraction, and division. We'll start with adding two numbers in different orders. In particular, you're going to compare the result when you compute 5 + 6 with the result when you compute 6 + 5. Form a group of 5 blocks and a group of 6 blocks. Add the group of 6 blocks to the group of 5 blocks. Count the number of blocks in the final group. Now place the blocks back in the original groups and add them together in a different order, meaning add the group of 5 blocks to the group of 6 blocks. Do you get the same answer either way? Sure. See Figure 1.17.

Figure 1.17

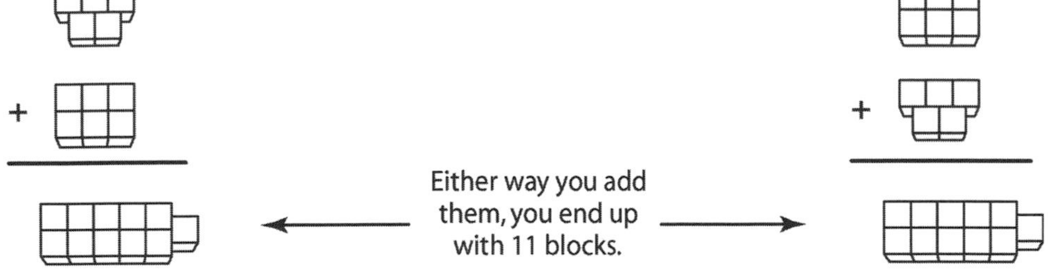

Either way you add them, you end up with 11 blocks.

Now you're going to multiply two numbers, changing the order of multiplication. In particular, you are going to compare 3 · 5 with 5 · 3. Create 3 groups of 5 blocks each and 5 groups of 3 blocks each, as in Figure 1.18. Add the total number of blocks in each case. Do you end up with the same total number of blocks in each case? Yep.

> **Guidepost** Using blocks to see what happens when you change the order of numbers in multiplication.

Figure 1.18

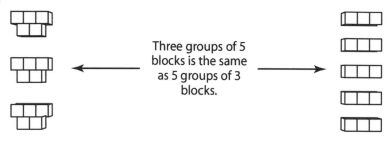

Three groups of 5 blocks is the same as 5 groups of 3 blocks.

Next we're going to see what happens when you change the order in subtraction. You'll use blocks to compare 8 – 5 with 5 – 8. Form a group of 8 blocks and take away (subtract) 5 blocks from this group. What do you end up with? Now that you've done that, form a group of 5 blocks and take away (subtract) 8 blocks from this group. What? Can't do it? Well no, you can't!* See Figure 1.19.

Figure 1.19

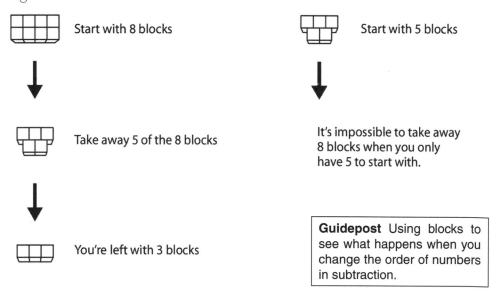

Start with 8 blocks

Start with 5 blocks

Take away 5 of the 8 blocks

It's impossible to take away 8 blocks when you only have 5 to start with.

You're left with 3 blocks

> **Guidepost** Using blocks to see what happens when you change the order of numbers in subtraction.

_____

* You probably are familiar with negative numbers, but we're not dealing with those yet.

Time to see what happens when you reverse order in dividing. You're going to compare $15 \div 3$ with $3 \div 15$. Divide a group of 15 blocks into groups of 3 each, as in Figure 1.20. No problem since you've done something like this in a previous section. Now divide a group of 3 blocks into groups of 15 each. Again, impossible if you don't break the blocks into pieces.

> **Guidepost** Using blocks to see what happens when you change the order of numbers in division.

Next we're going to investigate what happens when you don't change the order, but rather change the grouping, in math operations. As before, we're going to start with addition. You're going to compare adding 4 and 5, and then adding 6; with adding 5 and 6, and then adding 4. Form groups of 4, 5, and 6 blocks. Add the first two groups together, and then add the third group to these two. What's the result? Now return the blocks to their original groups of 4, 5, and 6. This time add the last two groups first, and then add the first group to them. What's the result? See Figure 1.21.

Figure 1.20

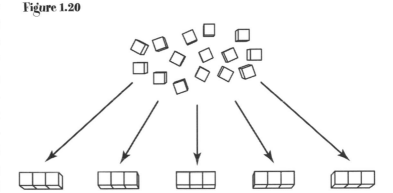

It's possible to divide 15 blocks into groups of 3.

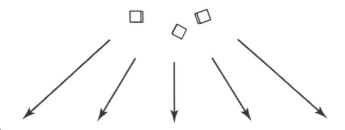

You can't divide 3 blocks into groups of 15 unless you break the blocks apart.

> **Guidepost** Using blocks to see what happens when you change the grouping of numbers in addition.

Figure 1.21

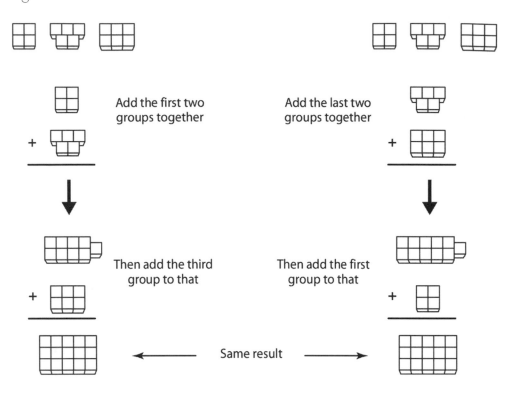

Add the first two groups together

Add the last two groups together

Then add the third group to that

Then add the first group to that

Same result

Switching to multiplication, you're going to investigate what happens when you multiply the numbers 3, 5, and 2 together, using different groupings. Create 3 groups of 5 blocks each and add them together (this corresponds to multiplying 3 by 5). You should end up with a group of 15. Add another group of 15 blocks to this one (this corresponds to multiplying the result of 3 · 5 by 2—remember that multiplication is repeated addition, so 15 · 2 is the same as 15 + 15). You end up with 30, right? Okay, now form 5 groups of 2 blocks each and add these together, ending up with 10 blocks (this corresponds to multiplying 5 by 2). Add 2 more groups of 10 blocks to these (this corresponds to multiplying the result of 5 · 2 by 3, or adding 10 three times). 30 again, right? Check out Figure 1.22.

Guidepost Using blocks to see what happens when you change the grouping of numbers in multiplication.

Figure 1.22

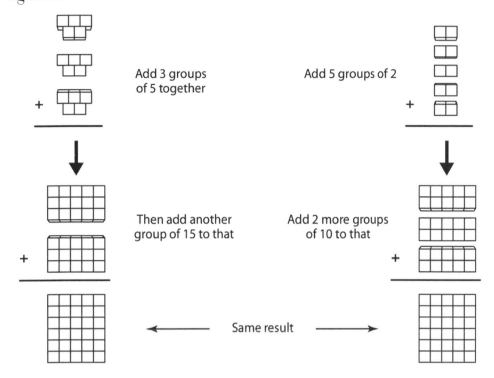

Add 3 groups
of 5 together

Add 5 groups of 2

Then add another
group of 15 to that

Add 2 more groups
of 10 to that

Same result

Guidepost Using blocks to see what happens when you change the grouping of numbers in subtraction.

OK, it's time to see what happens when you change grouping when subtracting. Start with a pile of 8 blocks. Subtract 4 blocks from this pile, and then subtract 3 blocks from the result. You should end up with 1 block, as shown in Figure 1.23. Then start with 4 blocks, subtract 3 blocks, and subtract the result from 8 blocks. This is also shown in Figure 1.23, and you should end up with 7 blocks.

What's next? Oh yeah, division. Let's see what happens when you use different groupings in division. Start with a group of 16 blocks and divide it into piles of 4. How many groups do you end up with? Yep, 4 groups. This tells us that 16 ÷ 4 = 4. We're now going to divide our result by two, so take a group of 4 blocks and divide it into groups of 2. How many groups of 2 do you have? Give yourself an A if you get an answer of 2.

Figure 1.23

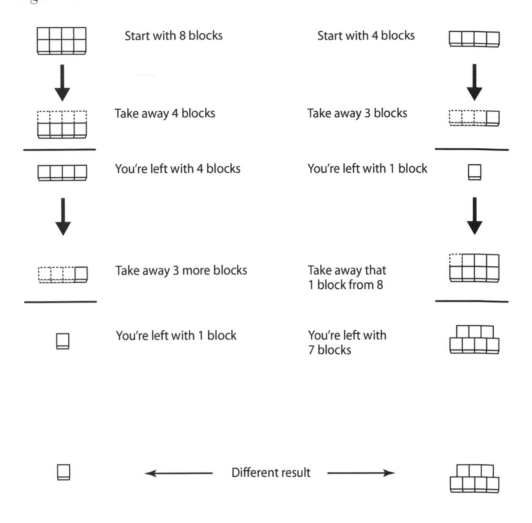

Start with 8 blocks	Start with 4 blocks	
Take away 4 blocks	Take away 3 blocks	
You're left with 4 blocks	You're left with 1 block	
Take away 3 more blocks	Take away that 1 block from 8	
You're left with 1 block	You're left with 7 blocks	

Different result

Guidepost Using blocks to see what happens when you change the grouping of numbers in division.

Let's start the division over by dividing 4 blocks into groups of 2. How many groups do you have? Two is correct. This corresponds to the operation 4 ÷ 2 = 2. Now divide a group of 16 blocks by our result of 2. In other words, separate the 16 blocks into 2 groups, and count how many blocks are in each group. Yep, 8. See Figure 1.24, and rest assured that all of this will make sense after you read the next section. Honest.

Figure 1.24

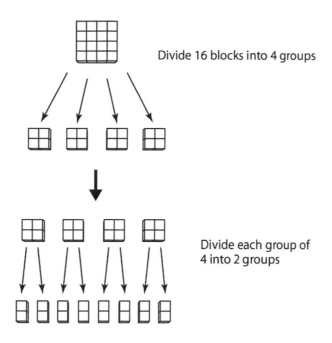

Divide 16 blocks into 4 groups

Divide each group of 4 into 2 groups

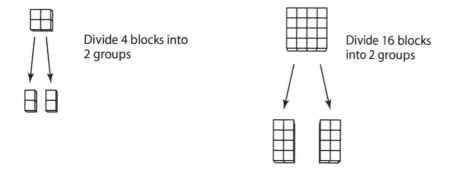

Divide 4 blocks into 2 groups

Divide 16 blocks into 2 groups

One final thing to do, or at least to imagine doing. I'll describe what to do, but it's a fair amount of trouble to actually carry out, so no demerits if you just think about doing it. Get two empty boxes, a sheet of paper, and a can of spray paint. Cut the paper into 20 equal-size pieces. Head outside and place 10 pieces of paper beside each box. Spray paint 10 of the pieces individually and then place them in one of the boxes. Place the 10 unpainted pieces into the second box and then spray paint them while they're in the box, with one sweeping motion. Note that in each case you end up with a box full of spray painted pieces of paper. If you hadn't seen the process, would you be able to tell which pieces were painted individually and which pieces were painted after they were in the box? Probably not, as long as you ignore any paint that missed the pieces of paper and might have gotten on the inside of the second box. See Figure 1.25. Yes, this does seem like a pretty silly thing to do!

Figure 1.25

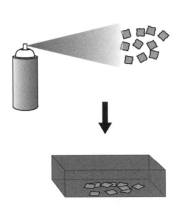

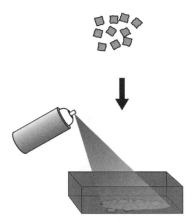

Individually spray paint 10 pieces of paper and then put them in a box.

Put 10 pieces of paper in a box, *then* spray paint them.

And even more explanation

> **Guidepost** An explanation of the commutative property of addition—order doesn't matter when adding.

That odd collection of activities I just had you do illustrates a few important properties about how numbers behave. The first is that when adding numbers, order doesn't matter. As illustrated in Figure 1.17, 5 + 6 gives you the same result as 6 + 5. Similarly, 213 + 766 is equal to 766 + 213. The name given to this fact is the **commutative property of addition**.

> **Guidepost** An explanation of the commutative property of multiplication—order doesn't matter when multiplying.

This property of numbers comes as no great surprise to people, just as the **commutative property of multiplication** is no big surprise. As you saw in Figure 1.18, 3 · 5 is equal to 5 · 3. The order in which you multiply things just doesn't matter—you always get the same result.

There is, however, no commutative property for subtraction or for division. In Figures 1.19 and 1.20, you saw that 8 − 5 is not the same as 5 − 8, nor is 15 ÷ 3 the same as 3 ÷ 15. Big deal, right? Well, yeah, it does become a big deal when you start working with variables (those letters that substitute for numbers), and it's not obvious that there are no commutative properties for subtraction and division. If you ever get confused about that fact when working with variables, you can always check things out using numbers or even blocks.

Guidepost An explanation that there is no commutative property for subtraction and division—order *does* matter in these operations.

In Figures 1.21 and 1.22, you saw a different property for both addition and multiplication, namely that it doesn't matter how you *group* numbers when adding or multiplying. The activity prior to Figure 1.21 illustrates that (4 + 5) + 6 gives you the same result as 4 + (5 + 6). And here, I have to explain how parentheses are used in math. Whenever you enclose an expression in parentheses, that's an instruction to do what's inside the parentheses first. So, 4 + (5 + 6) means you should add the 5 and 6 before you add the 4. The fact that you can group things any way you want and still get the same answer when adding is called the **associative property of addition**.

Guidepost An explanation of the associative properties of addition and multiplication—grouping doesn't matter in these operations.

The activity just prior to Figure 1.22 illustrates that you can group things any way you want when multiplying and still get the same answer. In that example, you saw that (3 · 5) · 2 is equal to 3 · (5 · 2). Not surprisingly, this is called the **associative property of multiplication**. In the activities associated with Figures 1.22 and 1.24, you found that there *isn't* an associative property for subtraction or division. With those operations, how you group things *does* matter. (8 − 4) − 3 is not the same as 8 − (4 − 3), and (16 ÷ 4) ÷ 2 is not the same as 16 ÷ (4 ÷ 2). Of course, it's fine to group numbers any way you want in subtraction and division, as long as you realize that you won't get the same answer with different groupings.

> **Guidepost** An explanation, using a physical analogy, of the distributive property, which deals with multiplying things inside parentheses by a quantity that's outside the parentheses.

Finally, you did (or thought about) that activity spray painting pieces of paper. In one case, you spray painted 10 separate pieces of paper and then added them together in a box. In another, you added the separate pieces of paper into the box first, and then spray painted them. The final result is the same, though. You end up with 10 painted pieces of paper in a box. This illustrates something called the **distributive property**. With numbers, it looks like $4 \cdot (3 + 2 + 6) = 4 \cdot 3 + 4 \cdot 2 + 4 \cdot 6$. Adding 3, 2, and 6 together before multiplying by 4 is like putting the pieces of paper in the box and then spray painting them. Multiplying the 3, 2, and 6 each by 4 and *then* adding them together is like spray painting the pieces individually and then putting them in the box. If you do the calculation, you'll find that $4 \cdot (3 + 2 + 6)$ is equal to 44, and $4 \cdot 3 + 4 \cdot 2 + 4 \cdot 6$ is also equal to 44.

That's it for the first chapter. Keep in mind that I'm illustrating the difference between knowing the rules of math and understanding the *meaning* behind the rules of math. It's best to start with simple things when illustrating that difference. I'm going to apply the same idea to increasingly more complex (complex on the surface, at least) concepts in math, including geometry, trigonometry, and even calculus.

Chapter Summary

- There are many different number systems one can use for counting, adding, multiplying, and so on. We commonly use the Base 10 system, but Base 2, Base 5, Base 7, or any other base, is possible.

- We "carry" and "borrow" numbers when using shorthand notation for addition and subtraction because the shorthand notation involves grouping objects into specific categories or place values.

- Multiplication is a convenient way to represent repeated addition.

- Division is, conceptually, the reverse of multiplication and can also be thought of as repeated subtraction.

- The order of terms doesn't matter in addition or multiplication. The names for these properties are the commutative property of addition and the commutative property of multiplication.

- The grouping of terms doesn't matter in addition or multiplication. The names for these properties are the associative property of addition and the associative property of multiplication.

- There are no commutative or associative properties for subtraction and division—order and grouping *do* matter in these operations.

- The distributive property describes the proper way to deal with terms outside parentheses multiplying a sum of terms inside the parentheses.

Applications

1. You might be wondering why in the world we mess with bases other than Base 10. It's the base everyone in the world uses, right? Well, no. Base 2 is also a popular base to use, because numbers in Base 2 consist only of ones and zeroes. It turns out that that ones and zeroes are pretty easy to represent with electric circuits, and electric circuits are what computers are made of. Therefore, the language of computers is binary math.[*]

2. How do you figure out what a math expression equals? For example, suppose you have 4 + 3 · 5 · (8 – 3) ÷ 5. Which operation do you perform first, second, third, and so forth? It's really an arbitrary choice. As long as everyone agrees on the order in which you perform operations, it doesn't matter what that order is. Fortunately, mathematicians long ago decided what that order should be. You perform any operations inside parentheses first, followed by any exponents in the expression,[†] followed by multiplication and division, followed by addition and subtraction. There's a mnemonic for remembering this order of operations—**PEMDAS**. When you use this mnemonic, you have to remember that multiplication and division are on equal footing, and addition and subtraction are on equal footing, which means that if you encounter a subtraction followed by an addition, you perform whichever operation comes first, going from left to right. Let's apply this order of operations to the expression 4 + 3 · 5 · (8 – 3) ÷ 5. First we do what's inside the parentheses (subtract 3 from 8) and end up with 4 + 3 · 5 · 5 ÷ 5. Next we do multiplication and division ahead of addition and subtraction, and we do those in order from left to right. So, the next thing to do is multiply the 3 by the 5, resulting in 4 + 15 · 5 ÷ 5. The addition still waits until last, so the next thing to do is multiply 15 by 5, resulting in 4 + 75 ÷ 5. Next we

---

[*] See the *Stop Faking It!* book on Electricity and Magnetism for how to use electrical circuits to model binary math.

[†] No, we haven't discussed exponents yet.

do the division and get 4 + 15. Finally we do the addition and get 19. By the way, there's an expression for remembering PEMDAS, which is Please Excuse My Dear Aunt Sally. Personally, I hate that expression, as I'm not sure what Aunt Sally did to require us to excuse her, and even if we did know what she did, I'm not sure I would decide to excuse her.

At the Mnemonics Institute

Fractions and More Rules

This chapter deals with fractions and decimals. This is one place where people who are otherwise fine with math jump off the boat and decide it's just too weird to continue. As with everything else, though, it's only a matter of understanding what's going on. Try to memorize your way through, and you're in trouble. Insist that everything makes sense, though, and you're fine.

Rose dreaded the Math Club's "Pizza Night."

Things to do coupled with explanations

I usually have "things to do" sections followed by "explanation" sections. This chapter doesn't lend itself to that format, so rather than separate the things to do from the explanation, it will be easier to understand if we explain as we go along.

For starters, take a look at the circles below in Figure 2.1. In fact, you should make a copy of this page, because you're going to be cutting the circles out and you probably don't want to ruin the book.

Figure 2.1

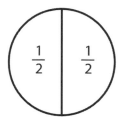 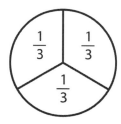 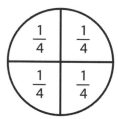

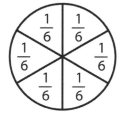 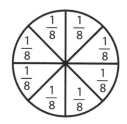 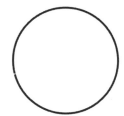

Each circle, except for the blank one, is divided into fractional pieces. For example, the second one is divided into three equal-sized pieces we call thirds. Each section is one third of the whole circle, and we write that fraction as $\frac{1}{3}$. This is a physical representation of a fraction, and this representation is the one most people think of when they think of fractions. It's pretty easy to picture one-half of an apple, one-fourth of a glass of water, or two-fifths of a candy bar. Fractions also represent the procedure of division, though. The fraction $\frac{1}{3}$ is the number one divided by the number three, so $\frac{1}{3}$ is the same as $1 \div 3$.

Guidepost Different ways to picture fractions.

Previously we pictured division as separating a large collection of blocks into smaller groups, but here we have the number 1, which would be 1 block, divided into three groups. In order to do that, we have to break the block into smaller pieces. That's essentially what the second circle in Figure 2.1 shows. You can't divide one circle into three groups of circles, but you can divide it into three separate pieces. Figure 2.2 compares everyday division with the division represented by a fraction.

Figure 2.2

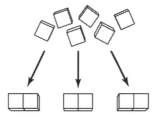

Dividing the number 6 by 3
Each group has two blocks.

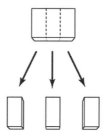

Dividing the number 1 by 3
Each piece has a size of $\frac{1}{3}$.

OK, what about a fraction like $\frac{2}{3}$? How do you divide two whole things into three "groups?" Pretty much the same way you divide one thing into three groups, or rather pieces. Figure 2.3 shows two circles divided into three equal groups. Each group contains two pieces of size $\frac{1}{3}$, and represents two divided by three, or $\frac{2}{3}$.

Figure 2.3 shows that a piece of a circle that has a size of $\frac{2}{3}$ is equivalent to two pieces with size $\frac{1}{3}$. This again points out the different ways we can think of fractions. One is as a simple division (the number 2 divided by the number 3) and one is as a physical entity (a section whose size is equivalent to that of two pieces, each one-third in size).

Before moving on, I should explain the terminology used for fractions. Whatever is on the top of the fraction is

Figure 2.3

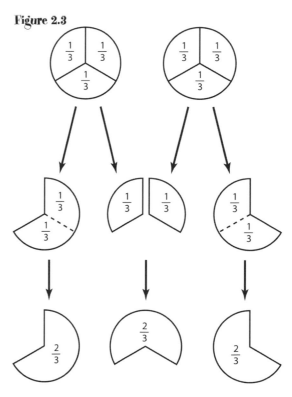

Each of these has a size of $\frac{2}{3}$.

called the **numerator** and whatever is on the bottom of the fraction is called the **denominator**.

Time to cut out all the circle pieces. Find a piece that is exactly half the size of a $\frac{1}{3}$ piece.

That would be a $\frac{1}{6}$ piece, as shown in Figure 2.4.

Figure 2.4

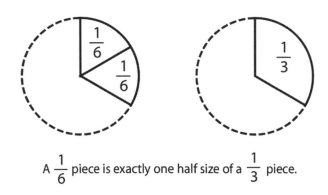

A $\frac{1}{6}$ piece is exactly one half size of a $\frac{1}{3}$ piece.

Guidepost The rule for multiplying fractions—making sense of it.

This illustrates that "half of $\frac{1}{3}$ is $\frac{1}{6}$." This also illustrates what it means to multiply fractions. Another way to represent "half of" something is to multiply the something by $\frac{1}{2}$. In other words, $\frac{1}{2} \cdot \frac{1}{3} = \frac{1}{6}$. This also tells us the rule for multiplying fractions. You multiply the numerators to get the numerator of the answer ($1 \cdot 1 = 1$) and you multiply the denominators to get the denominator of the answer ($2 \cdot 3 = 6$). And this also fits with our earlier representation of multiplication as a series of additions. $4 \cdot 5$ means add 5 four times. $\frac{1}{2} \cdot \frac{1}{3}$ means add $\frac{1}{3}$ one half of a time, or simply take one half of $\frac{1}{3}$.

Guidepost Understanding equivalent fractions and how to convert from a fraction to its equivalent.

When you multiply fractions in math problems, I'm not expecting that you'll break the process down like this. You will simply multiply the numerators and denominators, following the rule. You should always, however, be able to stop and explain *why* that's the proper rule. When teaching, you should stop every once in a while and ask the students *why* the rule makes sense. If they can't give an answer, then I suggest it would be worthwhile to stop and talk about the reasoning behind the rule. I further suggest that this would be appropriate all the way through the college level. Too often we think that illustrating fractions with pie slices and reasoning through rules is "baby stuff" that isn't appropriate once kids get to, say, the fifth grade and beyond. My position is that we don't do nearly enough of that baby stuff at all levels.

Take two of your $\frac{1}{6}$ pieces and place them on the second circle in Figure 2.1. Convince yourself that $\frac{2}{6}$, which is two pieces of size $\frac{1}{6}$, is equivalent to a piece of size $\frac{1}{3}$. Similarly, convince yourself that $\frac{1}{2}$ is equivalent to $\frac{3}{6}$, and that $\frac{3}{4}$ is equivalent to $\frac{6}{8}$. See Figure 2.5.

We can show that these fractions are equivalent just using math symbols. First, you have to recall that anything multiplied by 1 is just the thing you started with. So, you can multiply by 1 all day long and not change the value of a fraction. Second, you have to recall that anything divided by itself is equal to 1, as in $\frac{2}{2} = 1$, $\frac{5}{5} = 1$, and $\frac{a\ squid}{a\ squid} = 1$. Having recalled that, let's multiply the fraction $\frac{1}{3}$ by the number 1.

$$\frac{1}{3} \cdot 1 = \frac{1}{3}, \text{ right?}$$

Now let's rewrite the number 1 as $\frac{2}{2}$, which we can do because 2 divided by 2 is equal to 1. Now we have

$$\frac{1}{3} \cdot 1 = \frac{1}{3} \cdot \frac{2}{2}.$$

Using our rule for multiplying fractions, we have

$$\frac{1}{3} \cdot \frac{2}{2} = \frac{2}{6}.$$

This confirms what you discovered with the circle pieces, namely that $\frac{1}{3}$ and $\frac{2}{6}$ represent the same fraction. This also illustrates how we can change the denominator in a fraction while making sure the fraction has the same value. Just multiply by 1, disguised as a number divided by itself. For example, you saw with the circle pieces that $\frac{1}{2}$ is the same

Figure 2.5

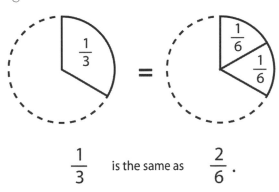

$\frac{1}{3}$ is the same as $\frac{2}{6}$.

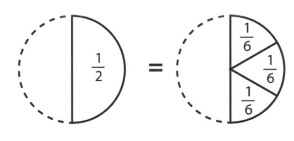

$\frac{1}{2}$ is the same as $\frac{3}{6}$.

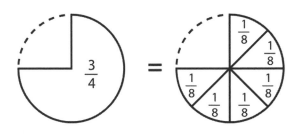

$\frac{3}{4}$ is the same as $\frac{6}{8}$.

as $\frac{3}{6}$. We can do the same thing by multiplying $\frac{1}{2}$ by $\frac{3}{3}$, as in

$$\frac{1}{2} \cdot \frac{2}{2} = \frac{3}{6}.$$

You also saw with the pieces that $\frac{3}{4}$ is equivalent to $\frac{6}{8}$, something we can do with math symbols as

$$\frac{3}{4} \cdot \frac{2}{2} = \frac{6}{8}.$$

OK, we've covered what fractions are, how to multiply fractions, and how to change the denominator of a fraction by multiplying the entire fraction by 1, disguised as a number divided by itself.

Let's move on to adding fractions, starting with the rule for doing so, which you can find in any math textbook.[*] The rule is that you need to get a common denominator for the fractions, followed by adding the numerators and keeping the denominators the same. Do you really need to get a common denominator, though?

Guidepost Understanding why you're supposed to get a common denominator when adding fractions.

Check it out using the circle pieces. On a blank circle, place a $\frac{1}{2}$ piece and a $\frac{1}{3}$ piece, as in Figure 2.6.

Figure 2.6

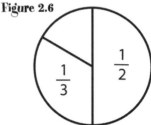

This is a physical representation of $\frac{1}{2} + \frac{1}{3}$, so clearly we *can* add fractions that have different denominators. There's a problem, though. Unless you have carefully drawn circles and can measure exactly the fraction of the circle taken up by these two pieces, you don't have an exact answer for $\frac{1}{2} + \frac{1}{3}$. See Figure 2.7.

Our problem, then, is that we can add fractions that have different denominators, but we don't necessarily arrive at an exact answer. We can, however, get an exact answer if the fractions have the same denominator. For example, $\frac{1}{6} + \frac{2}{6} = \frac{3}{6}$, which you can verify using your cut-out circles from Figure 2.1. This kind of fraction addition also makes common sense. If you have one of something (a sixth, in this case) and add two of those somethings

Figure 2.7

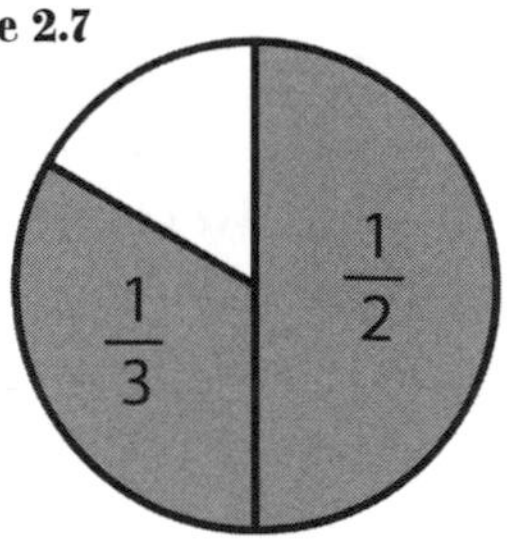

It's not obvious how much of the circle is shaded.

---

[*] In much of this book, I try to use activities to *develop* the rules of math. I'm starting with the rule this time for a change of pace, so you can see how we can justify the rule while making sure it makes sense. Of course, I'm also assuming you already know this rule, and many other rules, of math.

(two-sixths) to it, you end up with three of the somethings (or three-sixths).

The solution to the problem of adding fractions with unlike denominators, therefore, is to transform the fractions so they have a common denominator. We do that by multiplying each fraction by 1, disguised as one number divided by itself. Let's use that idea to tackle $\frac{1}{2} + \frac{1}{3}$.

If we multiply $\frac{1}{2}$ by $\frac{3}{3}$, we get $\frac{3}{6}$.

If we multiply $\frac{1}{3}$ by $\frac{2}{2}$, we get $\frac{2}{6}$.

Recalling that $\frac{3}{3}$ and $\frac{2}{2}$ are both equal to 1, and that multiplying anything by 1 doesn't change its value, we get

$$\frac{1}{2} + \frac{1}{3} = \frac{1}{2} \cdot \frac{3}{3} + \frac{1}{3} \cdot \frac{2}{2} = \frac{3}{6} + \frac{2}{6} = \frac{5}{6}$$

which means that our exact answer is $\frac{5}{6}$. You can verify this answer using pieces of a circle by placing the $\frac{1}{2}$ piece and the $\frac{1}{3}$ piece on the fourth circle in Figure 2.1 (the one divided into sixths). See Figure 2.8.

Figure 2.8

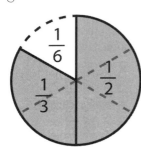

Just as with multiplication, I don't expect that you will go through this reasoning process each time you add fractions or ask your students to add fractions. I would suggest, however, asking students at any level of math, all the way up to college courses, *why* they have to get a common denominator when adding and subtracting fractions. I'm betting most won't know. You might get answers such as "because you can't add apples and oranges" or "because they have to be the same," but that's just restating the rule. Of course, you already know that you *can* add fractions without a common denominator (Figure 2.7). The only reason you need a common denominator is so you can get an exact answer.

The last thing I'm going to deal with in this section and in this chapter is the idea of using decimals rather than fractions. As you'll hopefully discover, decimals and fractions are just different notations for the same thing. Decimals really are fractions. To get started on this, let's expand our previous idea of place value in Base 10. Earlier, Base 10 place value was shown as in Figure 2.9.

Figure 2.9

> **Guidepost** Understanding decimals and their relationship to fractions.

This figure isn't complete, though, because as we all know, there is a decimal point and there are place values to the right of the decimal point. Figure 2.10 shows a more complete picture of Base 10 place value.

Figure 2.10

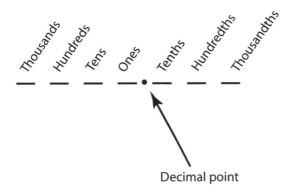

Decimal point

The places to the left of the decimal point represent ones, tens, hundreds, etc. The places to the right of the decimal point represent the fractions $\frac{1}{10}$, $\frac{1}{100}$, $\frac{1}{1000}$, etc. So, the number 456.291 means you have 4 thousands, 5 hundreds, 6 ones, 2 tenths, 9 hundredths, and 1 thousandth. If we were to represent this number using fractions rather than decimals, it would be 456 + $\frac{2}{10}$ + $\frac{9}{100}$ + $\frac{1}{1000}$. So, the only thing special about decimals is that they are shorthand for fractions, using Base 10.

OK, how do we go about converting a fraction like $\frac{3}{4}$ to a decimal? Well, we use the calculator and divide 3 by 4, ending up with 0.75. What might be more instructive, however, is to see what happens when we use long division. You remember long division, don't you? It's that process all of us used before calculators. Anyway, let's divide 3 by 4, using long division. We start with the following familiar look:

$$4\overline{)3}$$

Those symbols are basically asking you how many ones you get when you divide 3 by 4. The answer is that you don't get any ones, because 3 divided by 4 is less than 1. The next step is to convert those 3 ones to 30 tenths, which means adding a decimal point and a zero to keep track of the fact that we're now dealing with tenths.

$$4\overline{)3.0}$$

Adding a zero means we have 30 tenths.

Now we're dividing 30 tenths by 4, asking how many groups of 4 tenths there are in 30 tenths. Well, there are 7 groups of 4 tenths in 30 tenths, with a couple of tenths left over. In our long division, it looks like

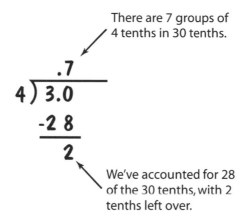

There are 7 groups of 4 tenths in 30 tenths.

We've accounted for 28 of the 30 tenths, with 2 tenths left over.

Now, since there are only 2 tenths left over, we can no longer divide them into groups of 4 tenths. Therefore, we rewrite the 2 tenths as 20 hundredths.

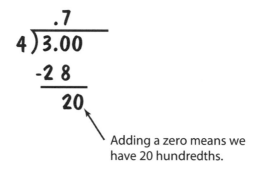

Adding a zero means we have 20 hundredths.

Now we're dividing 20 hundredths by 4, asking how many groups of 4 hundredths there are in 20 hundredths. The answer is 5, so we get

There are 5 groups of 4 hundredths in 20 hundredths.

$$
\begin{array}{r}
.75 \\
4\overline{)3.00} \\
-2\ 8 \\
\hline
20 \\
-20 \\
\end{array}
$$

$$
\begin{array}{r}
.75 \\
4\overline{)3.00} \\
-2\ 8 \\
\hline
20 \\
-20 \\
\hline
0 \\
\end{array}
$$

We're done, because there are no hundredths left over. We've converted the fraction three-fourths to seven-tenths plus 5 hundredths. See Figure 2.11.

Figure 2.11

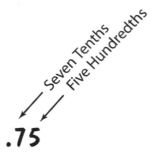

And that's all there really is to converting fractions to decimals. Converting decimals to fractions is also pretty easy. 0.75 is 7 tenths and 5 hundredths, or $\frac{75}{100}$. Most math books cover pretty well what comes next, which is the process of "reducing fractions." We can rewrite $\frac{75}{100}$ as $\frac{3 \cdot 25}{4 \cdot 25}$ which, by the reverse of our rule for multiplying fractions, is equal to $\frac{3}{4} \cdot \frac{25}{25}$. Because $\frac{25}{25}$ is equal to 1, this expression is equal to $\frac{3}{4}$. By the way, this is the process behind the procedure known as "canceling." Because we can remove the $\frac{25}{25}$ from the above expression by using the reverse of fraction multiplication, we can take a shortcut and just cancel the 25s, as in $\frac{3 \cdot \cancel{25}}{4 \cdot \cancel{25}}$.

Chapter Summary

- You can picture fractions as portions of a whole or as simple representations of division.

- You do not change the value of a fraction, or any other term for that matter, when you multiply it by the number 1.

- Anything divided by itself is equal to 1.

- When you multiply fractions, you multiply the numerators and multiply the denominators. There's a reason for that procedure.

- You *can* add fractions that have unlike denominators, but to get an exact answer you must first find a common denominator for the fractions.

- Decimals are a way of representing fractions and mixed numbers with Base 10 notation.

Applications

1. There's a rule for converting mixed numbers, such as $4\frac{2}{3}$, to what is called an "improper fraction." What you do is, in this case, multiply the 3 and 4, add the 2, and put the result as a numerator over the denominator of 3. Thus, $4\frac{2}{3}$ is equal to $\frac{3\cdot4+2}{3}$, which is equal to $\frac{14}{3}$. OK, fine, but why is that the rule? Does it make sense? Yes, it does, but it takes a bit of thinking to figure it out. First, $4\frac{2}{3}$ is read "4 *and* $\frac{2}{3}$" or "$4 + \frac{2}{3}$." In order to add these together, you have to rewrite the 4 as a fraction with a denominator of 3. Since there are three 3s in the number 1, there are twelve 3s in the number 4. Therefore, you can write the number 4 as $\frac{12}{3}$. Now we add $\frac{2}{3}$ to the 4, which is $\frac{12}{3} + \frac{2}{3}$. We have a common denominator of 3, so we can write this as $\frac{12+2}{3}$, or $\frac{14}{3}$.

2. We covered the rule for multiplying fractions in this chapter, making sense of it, so this should be a simple application. Let's multiply $\frac{6}{1}$ by $\frac{1}{6}$. We multiply the numerators and multiply the denominators, so $\frac{6}{1}\cdot\frac{1}{6}=\frac{6\cdot1}{1\cdot6}=\frac{6}{6}$. Because we know that anything divided by itself is equal to 1, we know that $\frac{6}{6}$ is equal to 1. So, $\frac{6}{1}\cdot\frac{1}{6}$ is equal to 1. There is a special name for two numbers that, when multiplied together, equal 1. Those numbers are **reciprocals** of each other. Finding the reciprocal of a fraction is pretty easy. Just invert the fraction so the numerator and denominator are reversed, and you have the reciprocal. The reciprocal of $\frac{3}{8}$ is $\frac{8}{3}$. The reciprocal of $\frac{15}{27}$ is $\frac{27}{15}$. Reciprocals are a nice thing to know about when you start solving math equations.

3. In various science applications there's a procedure known as the "factor label method." It's a fancy name that describes how one changes units associated with quantities. For example, consider something like 62 hours. The "hours" represent the units associated with the number 62. Suppose we want to know how many seconds are equivalent to 62 hours. Well, first we can convert to minutes by multiplying 62 hours by the number 1, disguised as $\frac{60\text{ minutes}}{1\text{ hour}}$. This fraction is equal to 1 because 60 minutes and 1 hour are the same thing. So, we have 62 hours $\cdot\ \frac{60\text{ minutes}}{1\text{ hour}}$, or $\frac{(62\text{ hours})\cdot(60\text{ minutes})}{1\text{ hour}}$.

   Now we can rewrite the 62 hours as $62\cdot(1\text{ hour})$ and end up with $\frac{62\cdot(1\text{ hour})\cdot(60\text{ minutes})}{1\text{ hour}}$.

   The next thing to do is cancel the "1 hour" terms, because $\frac{1\text{ hour}}{1\text{ hour}}$ is equal to 1. We get $\frac{62\cdot(1\text{ hour})\cdot(60\text{ minutes})}{1\text{ hour}}$ or just $62\cdot(60\text{ minutes})$, which equals 3720 minutes. To convert this further to seconds, we multiply 3720 minutes by $\frac{60\text{ seconds}}{1\text{ minute}}$. Because there are 60 seconds in a minute, this again is the same as multiplying by 1. Just as with the hours units earlier, the minutes units now cancel, and we're left with $3720\cdot(60\text{ seconds})$, which equals 227,200 seconds.

Now, in using the "factor-label method," there's a shortcut way to do a conversion like this. You simply write 62 hours $\cdot \frac{60 \text{ minutes}}{1 \text{ hour}} \cdot \frac{60 \text{ seconds}}{1 \text{ minute}}$. The hours units and minutes units all cancel, you multiply all the numbers together, and you end up with units of seconds. Many students view this factor-label method as some kind of magic trick, but all you're doing is multiplying by the number 1, disguised as one quantity divided by an equivalent quantity, over and over. Let's convert 1000 miles to meters using the full-blown shortcut, and relying on the fact that there are 0.6 kilometers in a mile and 1000 meters in a kilometer.

$$1000 \text{ miles} \cdot \frac{0.6 \text{ kilometers}}{1 \text{ mile}} \cdot \frac{1000 \text{ meters}}{1 \text{ kilometer}}$$

$$\text{equals } 1000 \, \cancel{\text{miles}} \cdot \frac{0.6 \, \cancel{\text{kilometers}}}{1 \, \cancel{\text{mile}}} \cdot \frac{1000 \text{ meters}}{1 \, \cancel{\text{kilometer}}}$$

equals 600,000 meters.

4. I dealt with the multiplication of fractions in this chapter, but not the division of fractions. Check out any math book and you'll find that the rule for dividing by a fraction is to "invert and multiply." This means that if you have $\frac{4}{5} \div \frac{2}{3}$, you should invert the $\frac{2}{3}$ to form $\frac{3}{2}$, and then do the multiplication $\frac{4}{5} \cdot \frac{3}{2}$, resulting in $\frac{12}{10}$, or $\frac{6}{5}$, or $1\frac{1}{5}$. That's the correct answer, but why does this rule work? To understand, let's use a simpler example and use our "definition" of division involving separating things into piles of blocks or pieces of blocks.

$$\text{Consider } \tfrac{13}{2} \div \tfrac{1}{2}.$$

The rule says to invert the $\frac{1}{2}$ and multiply, meaning you end up with $\frac{13}{2}$ $\cdot \frac{1}{2}$, which equals 13. Let's see if that makes sense in terms of our earlier definition of division. When you divide $\frac{13}{2}$ by $\frac{1}{2}$, you are in essence asking how many $\frac{1}{2}$s there are in $\frac{13}{2}$. Well, there are 13 halves in $\frac{13}{2}$, so we end up with the answer we get by following the rule. When you're doing something more complicated like $\frac{4}{5} \div \frac{2}{3}$, ending up with $1\frac{1}{5}$, the process is harder to follow. The answer does make sense, though. Because $\frac{2}{3}$ is smaller than $\frac{4}{5}$, it makes sense that there should be more than one $\frac{2}{3}$ in the fraction $\frac{4}{5}$. As with many other math rules, "invert and multiply" is a useful shortcut. If you don't understand the reasoning behind this rule, though, then you really don't understand what you're doing. You are simply following rules for the sake of following rules.

5. Here's another rule. When you multiply a number by 10, you simply move the decimal point to the right one place. When you divide by 10, you move the decimal point to the left one place. Multiplying or dividing by 100

moves the decimal point two places, multiplying or dividing by 1000 moves the decimal point three places, and so on. Convenient rule, but why does it work? Because we use the Base 10 number system. Let's look at the number 23.74. Knowing our place values, we know that this number represents 2 tens + 3 ones + 7 tenths + 4 hundredths. If you multiply this number by 10, then you multiply the 2 tens (20) by 10, multiply the 3 ones (3) by 10, multiply the 7 tenths (0.7) by 10, and multiply the 4 hundredths (0.04) by 10. $20 \cdot 10$ is equal to 200 (add up 10 groups of 20 each), 3 times 10 is 30, 0.7 (which is the same as the fraction $\frac{7}{10}$) times 10 is equal to 7, and 0.04 (which is the same as the fraction $\frac{4}{100}$) times 10 is equal to $\frac{4}{10}$, or 0.4. We end up with the number represented by 2 hundreds, 3 tens, 7 ones, and 4 tenths. We write that as 237.4, which corresponds to moving the decimal point one place to the right in the number 23.74. I'll leave it up to you to figure out why dividing by 10 simply moves the decimal point one place to the right. And once again, we have a shortcut accompanied by the reasoning behind the shortcut. In case you can't tell, that's basically the theme of this book.

Loose Ends

his chapter contains more basic material. This material could have been part of the first two chapters, but I'm hoping to segment things so you don't think you have to absorb too much all at once. Keeping with the theme of the first two chapters, I will be discussing procedures for which you no doubt know all the rules, but might not understand the reasoning behind the rules.

On Friday nights the mathematicians would go out cubing.

Things to do before you read the explanation

- Multiply the number 3 by itself and record the result.

- Multiply the number 3 by itself and then multiply the result by 3 (in other words, compute 3 · 3 · 3), and record the result.

- Multiply 3 by itself a total of four times, as in 3 · 3 · 3 · 3, and record the result.[*]

- Multiply 3 by itself a total of five times, as in 3 · 3 · 3 · 3 · 3, and record the result.

Now do the following, which should be rather easy if you did what I just asked you to.

- Find a number that, when multiplied by itself, equals the number 9.

- Find a number that, when multiplied by itself four times, equals the number 81.

- Find a number that, when multiplied by itself five times, equals the number 243.

Just a couple more things to do.

- Multiply the number 3 · 3 by the number 3 · 3 and write down the result.

- Multiply the number 3 · 3 by the number 3 · 3 · 3 and write down the result.

The explanation

It's a pain to keep writing things like 3 · 3 · 3 · 3 or 7 · 7 · 7 · 7 · 7, and such calculations occur often enough that we have a shorthand notation for them, known as exponential notation. We write 3 · 3 · 3 · 3 as 3^4 and we write 7 · 7 · 7 · 7 · 7 as 7^5. In these examples, the 3 and the 7 are called the bases and the 4 and the 5 are called the **exponents**. You even have a special key on your calculator to calculate exponents. Simple enough, right? We read something like 3^4 as "3 to the fourth power" or just "3 to the fourth." It should make sense that 3^1 is equal to 3 and 7^1 is equal to 7.

OK, let's move to the second part of what you did in the previous section. I asked you to figure out what number multiplied by itself is equal to the number

---

[*] A phrase like "multiplied by itself four times" can be confusing. If you multiply a number by itself four times, does that mean something like 2 · 2 · 2 · 2, or does it mean 2 · 2 · 2 · 2 · 2? The first example has four numbers, and the second example has four multiplications. I'm going to use the convention that 2 · 2 · 2 · 2 is the number 2 multiplied by itself four times, because that helps us remember that there are four 2s. 2 · 2 · 2 · 2 · 2 is the number 2 multiplied by itself five times, even though there are only four multiplications.

"But, my mom says I'm not suppose to square!"

9. That's easy; it's just the number 3.* Again, we ask that question often enough in math that we have a special notation for it, namely the **radical**. We also have a special symbol, which is $\sqrt{}$. So, we can say that $\sqrt{9}$ = 3 reads "the radical of 9 is equal to 3." Fine, but what if you have a question such as "What number multiplied by itself five times equals the number 243?" If you did the calculations I asked you to, you know that the answer is 3.

We don't call this a radical, but instead call it the "fifth root" of 243. With a simple change to the radical symbol, we have a symbol for the fifth root. It's $\sqrt[5]{}$. So, we can say that $\sqrt[5]{243}$ = 3.†

There's a different way of expressing radicals or fifth roots or tenth roots, and it involves exponents. Instead of writing $\sqrt{9}$, you can write $9^{1/2}$, read "9 to the one-half power." Similarly, you can write $\sqrt[5]{243}$ as $243^{1/5}$. This might seem like a

---

* If you are proficient with negative numbers, then you undoubtedly know that -3 is also an answer to the question. We're not dealing with negative numbers yet, though. If you allow for both positive and negative answers to the question, then the symbol $\sqrt{}$ represents something called the **square root**. When you only allow positive answers to the question, then the proper term is **radical** rather than square root.

---

† If we were completely consistent with the symbols, the symbol for the radical would be $\sqrt[2]{}$, to indicate that you are looking for a number multiplied by itself. You will seldom see the radical symbol written this way, though, so just remember that the 2 is implied in the symbol $\sqrt{}$.

cryptic notation, but not if we recall what a fraction represents and what division is. $1 \div 5$, or $\frac{1}{5}$, means divide the number 1 into five equal-sized groups that, when added together, give you a result of 1. Now we have the $\frac{1}{5}$ as an exponent, though. Because it's an exponent, it has a slightly different meaning. Now $243^{1/5}$ means divide 243 into five equal-sized groups that, when *multiplied* together, give you the number 243. The answer is 3, so $243^{1/5} = 3$.

I'm planning on reserving all talk about negative numbers until the next chapter, but I'm going to make an exception here. What does it mean to write 4^{-2}? In other words, what do negative exponents mean? Well, a negative exponent is the **reciprocal** of the number with a positive exponent. As you might recall from the Applications section in the previous chapter, the reciprocal of a number is just the inverted fraction of a number. The reciprocal of $\frac{3}{4}$ is $\frac{4}{3}$. The reciprocal of $\frac{7}{2}$ is $\frac{2}{7}$. The reciprocal of 5 is $\frac{1}{5}$. If that last one doesn't make sense, remember that 5 and $\frac{5}{1}$ are the same number.

> **Guidepost**   The meaning of negative exponents.

Okay, back to 4^{-2}. I told you that a negative exponent means take the reciprocal of the number to the positive exponent, something that we'll justify in the next chapter. Let's rewrite 4^{-2} as $\frac{4^{-2}}{1}$, which we can do because anything divided by the number 1 just gives you back what you started with. The reciprocal of this number, after changing to the exponent so it's positive, is $\frac{1}{4^2}$, which is equal to $\frac{1}{16}$. Here are a couple more examples. 2^{-5} is equal to $\frac{1}{2^5}$, which is equal to $\frac{1}{32}$. 3^{-4} is equal to $\frac{1}{3^4}$, which is equal to $\frac{1}{81}$.

In the last part of the previous section, I had you multiply $3 \cdot 3$ by $3 \cdot 3$ and then multiply $3 \cdot 3$ by $3 \cdot 3 \cdot 3$. We could write those calculations as $3^2 \cdot 3^2$ and $3^2 \cdot 3^3$. You should have gotten answers of $3^2 \cdot 3^2 = 81$ and $3^2 \cdot 3^3 = 243$. Another way to write these is $3^2 \cdot 3^2 = 3^4$, and $3^2 \cdot 3^3 = 3^5$, which demonstrates the following rule:

Whenever you multiply two exponents with the same base, you simply add the exponents.

> **Guidepost**   Explanation of the rule for multiplying exponents that have the same base.

So, $3^2 \cdot 3^2 = 3^{(2+2)} = 3^4$ and $3^2 \cdot 3^3 = 3^{(2+3)} = 3^5$. You probably already know that rule, or perhaps if you haven't messed with exponents in a while, you might have to look up the rule. Of course you, or your students, might get confused from time to time. What happens when you have $2^5 \cdot 3^4$? Can you apply the rule to this calculation? Does this equal something like $(2 \cdot 3)^9$ or maybe $(2 + 3)^9$? The answer is no, and you can see that the answer is no by going back to the definition of what an exponent is. $2^5 \cdot 3^4$ is equal to $2 \cdot 2 \cdot 2 \cdot 2 \cdot 2 \cdot 3 \cdot 3 \cdot 3 \cdot 3$. Get out your calculator and convince yourself that $2 \cdot 2 \cdot 2 \cdot 2 \cdot 2 \cdot 3 \cdot 3 \cdot 3 \cdot 3$ is equal to neither $(2 \cdot 3)^9$ nor $(2 + 3)^9$. I use this example to point out that blindly applying a rule, or what you sort of remember as the rule, can get you into lots of trouble. If you forget what the rule is, go back to the definition of exponents and what it means to multiply two exponential numbers. It only takes a short time, and what's more, the rule should make sense to you. Once again, math is more than rules. It makes sense!

More things to do before you read more explanation

Multiply the number 4,580,000,000 by the number 398,000. Yeah, you might want to use a calculator. If you do this on a calculator, you'll get one of two results. One result is that you'll get an error message. In fact, the calculator might not even let you enter the number 4,580,000,000. The other result is that the calculator will display the number 1.82, followed by something like E 15. What the heck does that mean?

While you're pondering that question, try something else. Multiply the number 0.00000000029 by the number 0.00000078. You should run into the same kind of result. You'll either get an error message or something like E followed by a negative number. In this case, it would be the number 2.26 E -16.

To answer the previous question, what it means is that the resulting number is either too large or too small to display on the calculator, at least not without special notation. How about I tell you about the special notation?

More explanation

In the Applications section of Chapter 1, I discussed how multiplying a number by 10 or 100 or 1000 simply has the effect of moving the decimal point to the right. Then I explained why that shortcut works. It's because we use the Base 10 number system, where the place values are as shown in Figure 3.1. Note that I have shown the place values using regular numbers and using exponential notation.

Let's look at the number 400. Knowing what we know about place value, we can say that this number represents "four hundreds." We can represent one hundred

Figure 3.1

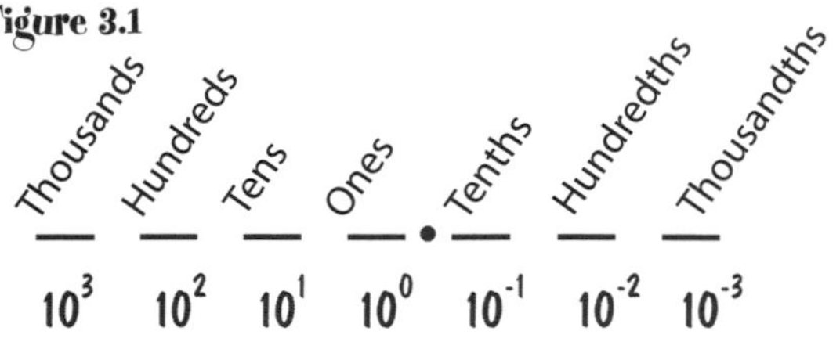

Thousands	Hundreds	Tens	Ones	Tenths	Hundredths	Thousandths
10^3	10^2	10^1	10^0	10^{-1}	10^{-2}	10^{-3}

> **Guidepost** Explanation of scientific notation and its uses.

in exponential notation as 10^2, and we can therefore represent four hundreds as $4 \cdot 10^2$. Similarly, we can represent 30,000 as $3 \cdot 10^4$. This is known as **scientific notation**. In textbooks and elsewhere, you might see these numbers as 4×10^2 and 3×10^4 or as 4 E 2 and 3 E 4. All those represent the same numbers in scientific notation, but I'm trying to be consistent in using a dot for multiplication in this book. The "E" notation is commonly used in calculators.

page 30 and check here ▶ 23b ☐			
dard deduction (see left margin).	24		$4 \mid 85 \times 10^5$
from line 22. If line 24 is more than line 22, enter -0-.	25		$9 \mid 48 \times 10^5$
7,025 or less, multiply \$3,100 by the total number of on line 6d. If line 22 is over \$107,025, see the age 32.	26		$31 \mid 10 \times 10^2$
from line 25. If line 26 is more than line 25, enter -0-. **table income.**	▶ 27		$9 \mid 17 \times 10^5$
any alternative minimum tax (see page 31).	28		$15 \mid 36 \times 10^2$
and dependent care expenses. e 2.	29		
Iderly or the disabled. Attach	30		
its. Attach Form 8863.	31		
ngs contributions credit. Attach	32	$78 \mid 36 \times 10^1$	
(see page 36).	33		
. Attach Form 8839.	34		
rough 34. These are your **total credits.**	35		$78 \mid 36 \times 10^1$
from line 28. If line 35 is more than line 28, enter -0-.	36		$145 \mid 76 \times 10^1$
d income credit payments from Form(s) W-2	37		
d 37. This is your **total tax.**	▶ 38		47944×10^4
by withhold from Forms W 2 and 1099	39	$25 \mid 28 \times 10^2$	

How a rocket scientist fills out his tax return form.

In Figure 3.1, you'll notice that the tenths place (to the right of the decimal point) is labeled with 10^{-1}. That's because 10^{-1} is equal to $1/10$. Likewise, the hundredths place is labeled with 10^{-2} and the thousandths place is labeled with 10^{-3}. OK, let's represent a small number with scientific notation. Because 0.004 is four thousandths, or $4/1000$, we can write it as $4 \cdot 10^{-3}$. We can even write more complicated numbers in scientific notation. If we multiply 0.000375 by 10,000, we get 3.75, and if we divide 3.75 by 10,000, we get the original number back, namely 0.000375. Therefore, we can write our original number as $3.75 \cdot 10^{-4}$.* If this makes sense to you, then you should be able to understand why we can write 412,000,000 as $4.12 \cdot 10^8$.

Well gosh, what's the point of scientific notation? Why use it? The reason we use scientific notation is that numbers in scientific applications can be very large or very small. For example, the mass of the Earth is 5,980,000,000,000,000,000,000,000

---

* To do these calculations, you can rely on the shortcut of moving the decimal point a certain number of places to the left or right. This is fine as long as you can, if necessary, stop and explain *why* multiplying by factors of 10 or dividing by factors of 10 causes the decimal point to move. In case you've already forgotten, go back to the Applications section of Chapter 2.

kilograms and the charge on an electron or proton is 0.00000000000000000016 coulombs. Sure is a whole lot easier to write these numbers as $5.98 \cdot 10^{24}$ kilograms and $1.6 \cdot 10^{-19}$ coulombs. Scientific notation also makes math manipulations a lot easier. In the beginning of the previous "things to do" section, I asked you to multiply 4,580,000,000 by 398,000. Let's write those in scientific notation as $4.56 \cdot 10^9$ and $3.98 \cdot 10^5$. Then our multiplication looks like

$$(4.56 \cdot 10^9) \cdot (3.98 \cdot 10^5)$$

Think back to Chapter 1 and things called the commutative property of multiplication and the associative property of multiplication. Those properties let us know that we can multiply things in any order and with any grouping. So, I'm going to change the order and the grouping of the above multiplication, indicating the grouping with parentheses.

$$(4.56 \cdot 3.98) \cdot (10^9 \cdot 10^5)$$

Next I'll do a couple multiplications, remembering that multiplying two exponents with the same base means you simply add the exponents. Our above multiplication now equals*

$$(18.1) \cdot (10^{14})$$

so we can write the answer as $18.1 \cdot 10^{14}$. It's customary to then write this as $1.81 \cdot 10^{15}$. That's a whole lot easier, and clearer, than keeping track of all those zeros in the original numbers, huh?

Of course, we can also divide using scientific notation. Let's divide the same numbers we just multiplied. We have

$$(4.56 \cdot 10^9) \div (3.98 \cdot 10^5)$$

which I'll write as $\frac{4.56 \cdot 10^9}{3.98 \cdot 10^5}$. Next I'll rewrite 10^9 as $10^5 \cdot 10^4$, which of course you understand because when you multiply numbers with the same base you add exponents. Now we have $\frac{4.56 \cdot 10^5 \cdot 10^4}{3.98 \cdot 10^5}$.

Because $\frac{10^5}{10^5}$ is equal to 1, we can cancel those terms[†] and get $\frac{4.56 \cdot \cancel{10}^5 \cdot 10^4}{3.98 \cdot \cancel{10}^5}$, which is equal to $\frac{4.56 \cdot 10^4}{3.98}$.

---

[*] If you do this calculation yourself, your calculator will no doubt give you the number 18.1488 rather than 18.1. Here I'm invoking a common practice in science of using only "significant figures." Numbers in science usually represent measurements that are only precise to a certain number of digits. When you multiply different measurements, you end up with numbers at the end that are essentially meaningless because they imply precision that isn't there, and the solution is to "crop" the final answer. Most high school science texts contain a detailed discussion of significant figures.

[†] Refer back to Chapter 2 for an explanation of canceling.

Now we can just divide the 4.56 by 3.98. That equals 1.15, so the final answer is $1.15 \cdot 10^4$. Once again, a lot easier than keeping track of all the zeros.

A Math Phobic's 10th worst nightmare: Soup du Jour is Number Soup.

Chapter Summary

- Exponents and exponential notation represent repeated multiplication.

- Taking the radical, the third root, the fourth root, and so on, of a number is the reverse of raising that number to a power. We can represent the radical, third, fourth, and all roots of a number with fractional exponents.

- A number raised to a negative exponent is equal to that number's reciprocal raised to the positive of the exponent.

- When you multiply two exponents that have the same base, the result is the base raised to the sum of the separate exponents.

- Scientific notation is a way of using exponents of the number 10 to represent very large and very small numbers.

Applications

1. In Chapter 1, I introduced you to the mathematical order of operations, represented by the mnemonic PEMDAS (Parentheses, Exponents, Multiplication, Division, Addition, Subtraction), which describes the convention people use to interpret math expressions. We can now add exponents to our previous description. First you do things inside parentheses,

then you do exponents, then you do multiplication and division (they're on an equal footing), and last you do addition and subtraction (also on an equal footing). Let's apply that to a simple expression like $(3 + 4)^2$. Because there is a procedure involving multiplication that is similar (see the next application), people sometimes think that $(3 + 4)^2$ is equal to $3^2 + 4^2$. Not true, though. We can apply PEMDAS to see that it's not true. Our rule says that things inside parentheses have to be done before exponents. That means you have to add the 3 and 4 to get 7, *then* square the result (multiply it by itself). That gives you 49, which is different from what you get by adding 3^2 and 4^2, which is 25.

2. OK, let's deal with what I referred to in the previous application, namely that the following calculation, or a calculation like it, is a legal move. $(4 \cdot 6)^3$ is equal to $4^3 \cdot 6^3$. Let's use what we know about exponents to figure this out. $(4 \cdot 6)^3$ is equal to $(4 \cdot 6) \cdot (4 \cdot 6) \cdot (4 \cdot 6)$. That's just using the definition of an exponent, along with our convention that parentheses are to be done before exponents. Now we already know that we can group things any way we want and change the order in multiplication. So, I'm going to change the order and the grouping of $(4 \cdot 6) \cdot (4 \cdot 6) \cdot (4 \cdot 6)$. I'm going to change it to $(4 \cdot 4 \cdot 4) \cdot (6 \cdot 6 \cdot 6)$. Well, $4 \cdot 4 \cdot 4$ is equal to 4^3 and $6 \cdot 6 \cdot 6$ is equal to 6^3, so we end up with $4^3 \cdot 6^3$. Therefore, $(4 \cdot 6)^3$ is equal to $4^3 \cdot 6^3$. Try this with any numbers you want, and it will always hold true.

3. Here's an example similar to the previous one. When you start dealing with radicals, you soon hear the following rule: *The radical of the product of several numbers is equal to the product of the individual radicals.* In case that description was just a bit too highbrow, let me illustrate with an example. $\sqrt{4 \cdot 9}$ is equal to $\sqrt{4} \cdot \sqrt{9}$. It's true for these particular numbers, because $\sqrt{4 \cdot 9} = \sqrt{36} = 6$, and $\sqrt{4} \cdot \sqrt{9} = 2 \cdot 3 = 6$. It's true in a more general sense, too. Instead of writing $\sqrt{4 \cdot 9}$, we can write $(4 \cdot 9)^{1/2}$. Now we have the product of two numbers raised to a power, which is just like Application 2. We can generalize from exponents that are integers[*] to exponents that are fractions. When we get to variables in Chapter 4, I'll try to demonstrate this rule in a more general sense.

4. It seems that there is much less emphasis on logarithms in math texts than there used to be, but they're still very useful in science especially, so I'll address them here and also later in the book when I talk about graphing. A logarithm is sort of the inverse of an exponent, but not exactly. To define a logarithm (or "log" for short), we simply ask the following question: log $(100) = ?$ The question this really asks is, "10 raised to what power equals 100?"

---

[*] In case this is a new term for you, *integer* refers to numbers such as -2, -1, 0, 1, 2, 3, 4, 5, etc., and doesn't include fractions.

So, implied in our question is that we're dealing with Base 10. To make that more explicit, we could write $\log_{10}(100) = ?$ We read that as "what is the log, base 10, of 100?" The answer in this case is pretty easy. $\log_{10}(100)$ is equal to 2, because 10 raised to the power of 2 is equal to 100. Similarly, $\log_{10}(1000)$ is equal to 3, because 10 to the third power equals 1000. I'll demonstrate the usefulness of logarithms in a later chapter.

Log-rhythms

5. There's a special kind of logarithm that is useful in both math and science. There is something called the *natural log*, which is a logarithm using a base other than Base 10. The base for this special kind of logarithm is Base e, where e is a special number in math that's sort of like the number represented by π. You might run into expressions such as *ln* 2 or e^x, where *ln* refers to the natural log, and e^x is just the number e raised to some power. No, that didn't help you understand natural logs very well, except to help you see that natural logs are just like regular logs, using a different base.

6. I mentioned that scientific models and explanations often use very large numbers and very small numbers. Here are some examples. The mass of the Sun is about $2 \cdot 10^{30}$ kilograms. The distance from the Earth to the nearest star (besides the Sun) is about $4 \cdot 10^{16}$ meters. The distance from the Earth to the edge of the known universe is around 10^{26} meters.[*] The mass of an electron is about $9 \cdot 10^{-31}$ kilograms. The distance across an atom is about 10^{-10} meters. The wavelength of visible light is around $5 \cdot 10^{-7}$ meters.

---

[*] This number changes from year to year as we get more information and have access to new theories about the content of the universe. Don't ever take this number as an unassailable "fact!"

Negative Influence

This chapter is all about negative numbers, and how to deal with them. They're not all that difficult to understand, but for some reason people get just a little uptight when they see computations involving negative numbers. I'm guessing that the apprehension results from the view that negative numbers mean there are more rules to follow—rules you don't necessarily understand. Well, we'll try and correct that.

"If you want to change, you have to think positive...or negative, negative."

Things to do before you read the explanation

Think about why we need negative numbers at all. Is there any place in your everyday life that you use negative numbers? If you need a few ideas, go on the internet and check out the range of elevations in New Orleans, the elevation of Death Valley, California, and the yearly temperature variations in Nome, Alaska. Of course you could just ask your kids for an example of where one uses negative numbers. My 11-year-old immediately answered, "Well, I guess in school, because I'm always owing people money."* Once you've convinced yourself that we use negative numbers all the time, try the following activity. Place a long (maybe 5 meters) piece of string or masking tape in a straight line on the floor. You could also go outside and draw a long, straight line in the dirt. Label the center of your line with a 0. Then make evenly spaced marks about a quarter of a meter apart to the right and left of the 0 mark. You should have something that looks like Figure 4.1.

Stand at the 0 mark and move four marks to the right. Label this mark with a 4. Then go back to the 0 mark and move four marks to the left.† Label this mark with a -4. You should now have something like Figure 4.2.

Go ahead and label all the other marks in the same fashion, with positive numbers to the right and negative numbers to the left, ending up with something like Figure 4.3.

Figure 4.1

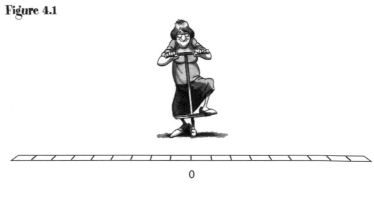

0

Figure 4.2

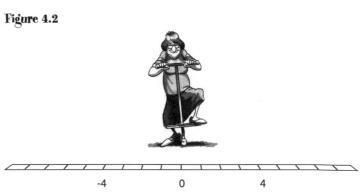

-4   0   4

---

* Don't get upset at me. He's talking about "class money" that he earns for classroom jobs and then spends on all sorts of junk that kids bring from home.

---

† As you do this, I'm assuming you are always facing the line in the same direction, so that right indicates one direction and left indicates the opposite direction. If you mix up right and left, you're going to have serious problems with this activity! Also, in the figures, since the woman is facing us, she moves in the opposite direction: Her left is your right and her right is your left, OK?

Next start at 0 and go stand by the number 7. Now do the opposite of what you just did (that means you start at 0 again). What number is at your feet? Start at 0 and go stand by the number -8, and then do the opposite of what you just did (starting at 0 again). Where are you?

Figure 4.3

More things to do, always starting at 0:

- Move to the right 5 marks and then move to the right 3 more marks. Where are you?

- Move to the right 5 marks and then move to the left 3 marks. Where are you?

- Move to the right 5 marks and then move to the left 9 marks. Where are you?

- Move to the left 3 marks and then move to the left 4 more marks. Where are you?

- Move to the left 3 marks and then move to the right 8 marks. Where are you?

- Move to the right 4 marks and then to the left 4 marks. Where are you?

- Move to the left 5 marks and then to the right 5 marks. Where are you?

- Move to the left 3 marks, then 3 marks more, then 3 marks more, then 3 marks more. Where are you?

Tired? Must be time for an explanation.

The explanation

If you looked up the elevations I asked you to, you should have found that the elevation of New Orleans varies from 1.5 meters below sea level to about 5 meters above sea level.* If we take sea level to be our "zero point," then the 1.5 is a negative number and the 5 is a positive number.

---

* Hurricane Katrina hit the Gulf Coast as I was revising this book. The real-life implications of having a negative elevation (below sea level) in New Orleans became quite apparent during this catastrophe.

If you looked up the temperatures in Nome, Alaska, then you should have come across negative temperatures, or temperatures below zero. Temperatures at any location that are below zero are negative numbers and temperatures that are above zero are positive numbers. Of course, whether the temperature is negative or positive often depends on the temperature scale you're using. Celsius temperatures are common for scientific purposes. In that scale, zero degrees is the temperature at which water freezes.

We run into negative numbers so often that it helps to have rules for dealing with them. Of course, one can understand why those rules make sense. That's where the activity involving moving to the right and left on the masking tape comes in.

> **Guidepost**   Using a number line to represent both positive and negative numbers.

What you constructed with your string or masking tape is a large-scale model of what is known as a **number line**. You'll see number lines in just about every math book you run across. There's usually a zero at the center, with positive numbers moving off to the right and negative numbers moving off to the left, as in Figure 4.4. The arrows on either end mean that this number line theoretically moves on forever in either direction.

Figure 4.4

A number line

You can represent all sorts of numbers on a number line, including fractions and strange numbers like e or π. For now, though, we'll stick with integers such as 1, 4, -3, and -7.[*]

> **Guidepost**   What it means to take the negative of a number.

Your physical number line, and a drawn number line, will help us understand all sorts of rules for dealing with both positive and negative numbers. One of the

---

[*] No doubt any textbook you use will make a big deal out of the different sets of numbers. The names *whole numbers, rational numbers, irrational numbers, real numbers, integers, natural numbers,* etc., are probably familiar. I'm not going to go out of my way to distinguish between these sets of numbers, though. You can find their descriptions and definitions just about anywhere if they become important to you.

first things I asked you to do in the previous "things to do" section was move from 0 to 7, and then do the opposite of that. When you did the opposite of moving to 7, you ended up at -7. That points out what a negative sign means. It means "do the opposite of" on the number line. The next thing I had you do in the previous section was move from 0 to -8 and then do the opposite of that action. You ended up at +8. So, the opposite of -8 is +8.

Let's do that last one in math symbols. Start with the number 8, which represents moving to +8 on the number line.[*] To get to the opposite side of the number line, you write -8. To go again to the opposite side of the number line, you write –(-8). Thus, the negative of a negative is a positive. We can also write –(-8) as (-1) · (-8), because 1 times anything is the anything.[6] Because we know that (-1) · (-8) is equal to 8, this illustrates a common rule of math, which is that *a negative times a negative equals a positive*. See Figure 4.5.

> **Guidepost** Why a negative times a negative equals a positive.

Figure 4.5

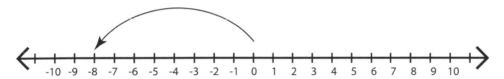

-8 means moves eight places to the left.

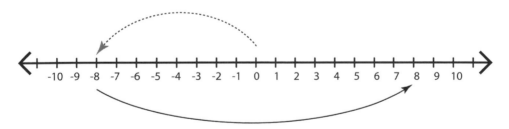

-(-8) means do the opposite of the first action. That puts you at +8.

---

[*] If there isn't a plus or minus sign in front of a number, the number is assumed to be positive. So, 8 and +8 represent the same number.

---

[6] In case writing –(-8) as (-1) · (-8) confuses you, here are a couple of intermediate steps. Because 1 times anything is the anything, -(-8) is equal to –[1 · (-8)]. Now we can just associate the negative sign out front with the 1, and get (-1) · (-8).

Moving on, I had you move five marks to the right and then three marks farther to the right. This illustrates simple addition, as in 5 + 3. Figure 4.6 shows this.

Figure 4.6

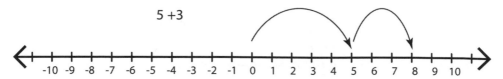

5 +3

Move five places to the right. Then move three more places to the right.

Next I had you move five marks to the right and then three marks to the left, ending up at the mark labeled 2. This illustrates simple subtraction and also another "rule" when adding and subtracting positive and negative numbers. 5 – 3 is the same as 5 + (-3). Five plus three would put you at the number 8, but five plus "the opposite of 3" puts you at the number 2. See Figure 4.7.

Figure 4.7

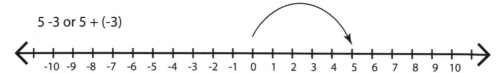

5 -3 or 5 + (-3)

Starting with 5 means moving to the right five places.

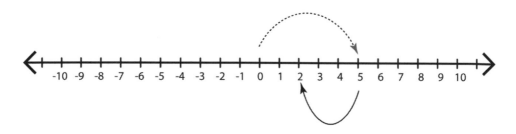

Subtracting 3 from 5 means moving to the left three places.
Adding a (-3) also means moving to the left three places.

Guidepost Why subtraction is the same as adding the opposite.

The next task was to move five marks to the right and then nine marks to the left. This illustrates the computation 5 – 9, or 5 + (-9), as shown in Figure 4.8.

Figure 4.8

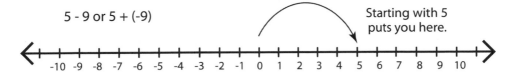

5 - 9 or 5 + (-9)   Starting with 5 puts you here.

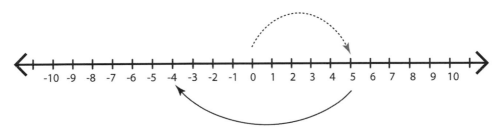

Subtracting 9 means moving to the left nine places.
Adding a (-9) also means moving to the left nine places. You end up at -4.

Guidepost The meaning of adding and subtracting numbers when one or both are negative.

Moving three marks to the left and then another four marks to the left illustrates the computation -3 – 4, or -3 + (-4). See Figure 4.9.

Figure 4.9

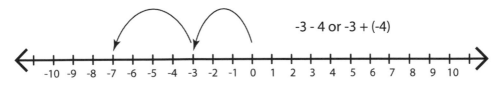

-3 - 4 or -3 + (-4)

-3 means moving to the left three places.
Subtracting 4, or adding (-4), means moving to the left four more places.

Next you moved three marks to the left followed by eight marks to the right, ending up at +5. That represents the calculation -3 + 8, shown in Figure 4.10.

Figure 4.10

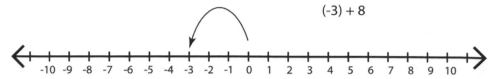

(-3) + 8

(-3) means move to the left three places.

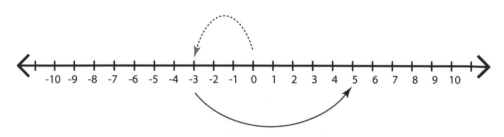

+8 means then move to the right eight places.

This gives me a chance to address another "shortcut" sometimes used when adding numbers of unlike signs. What you're supposed to do is subtract the smaller number from the larger number, and then assign the sign (+ or -) of the larger number to the result. Thus, with -3 + 8, you subtract the 3 from the 8 and then make it positive because the 8 is positive. With 5 – 9, otherwise written as 5 + (-9), you subtract the 5 from the 9 and make the result negative because the 9 is negative. I'm not a big fan of that shortcut, though, because it's a bit of a mindless procedure.* If you simply picture things on a number line you'll never go wrong.

Okay, on to the next two procedures. I had you start at zero, move to the right four marks, and then move to the left four marks. Then I had you start

---

> **Guidepost** Illustrating the fact that adding a number to its negative gives you zero as a result.

---

* This shortcut *does* have a solid foundation and it works. It just seems to me easier to take a different route. If you commonly use this technique, don't let me stop you!

at zero, move to the left 5 marks, and then move to the right 5 marks. In both cases, you end up at zero, as in Figure 4.11.

Figure 4.11

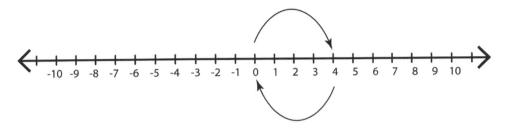

(+4) means move to the right four places.
Subtracting 4 puts you back at 0.

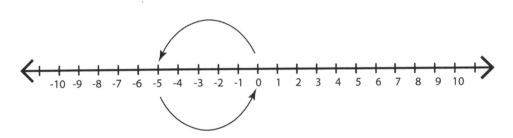

(-5) means move to the left five places. Adding five puts you back to 0.

Mathematically, we write these as 4 – 4 = 0 and -5 + 5 = 0. These are examples of what is often referred to as the additive inverse, which basically refers to the fact that a number added to its **additive inverse** is equal to zero. The additive inverse of 4 is -4, and the additive inverse of -4 is 4. This might not seem like a big deal, but it becomes a big deal when you start solving equations. In solving equations, you often look for the additive inverse of something in the hopes of making something equal to zero, resulting in it disappearing from one side of the equation or another. More on that in a later chapter.

The last thing I had you do was move three marks to the left, three marks more, three marks more, and three marks more. You ended up at the number -12. This illustrates the multiplication of 4 · (-3). So, 4 · (-3) = -12. So what? You already knew that, because 4 · 3 = 12, and a positive times a negative equals a negative. The key here is that you now know *why* a positive times a negative equals a negative. You are adding up a negative number a positive number of times, so you keep moving to the left on the number line. See Figure 4.12.

> **Guidepost** Explaining what it means to multiply a negative number by a positive number, and what it means to multiply a negative number by a negative number.

Figure 4.12

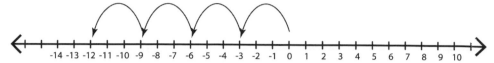

4 · (-3) means move to the left three places, and do it four times.

So far, we've covered why a positive times a negative gives you a negative, why a negative times a negative gives you a positive, why subtracting a number is the same as adding the negative of the number, and why addition and subtraction using positive and negative numbers makes sense. I'll expand on this a bit in the Applications section. Now, though, it's time to do more activities.

More things to do before you read more explanation

I know you're really tired from all that moving around on the number line, so I'll give you a few sedentary activities to do. For maximum benefit, try to figure these things out before you read the later explanation.

- We dealt with multiplying numbers with exponents in the previous chapter, but we never talked about dealing with exponents that were all negative. What do you suppose $5^{-3} \cdot 5^{-4}$ equals?

- What is $\sqrt[3]{-8}$, or $(-8)^{1/3}$, equal to?

- What is $\sqrt{16}$? That's a trivial answer if we read $\sqrt{16}$ as the *radical* of 16, because that means only positive answers are allowed. Since we're dealing with negatives now, does your answer change if you allow the answer to be negative?

- What is $\sqrt{-1}$ equal to? Yep, that's a puzzler.

More explanation

Let's start with the first question, shall we? We dealt with multiplying numbers with exponents in the previous chapter, but we never talked about dealing with exponents that were all negative. *What do you suppose $5^{-3} \cdot 5^{-4}$ equals?* This one probably wasn't too difficult for you. We can simply apply our rule that when you multiply exponents with the same base, you add the exponents. Adding -3 and -4 gives you -7, so the answer is 5^{-7}. Of course, we can also convert these to reciprocals with positive exponents so the process makes sense.

$5^{-3} = \dfrac{1}{5^3}$ and $5^{-4} = \dfrac{1}{5^4}$,

so $5^{-3} \cdot 5^{-4}$ is equal to $\dfrac{1}{5^3} \cdot \dfrac{1}{5^4}$,

which equals $\dfrac{1}{5^3 \cdot 5^4}$,

which equals $\dfrac{1}{5^7}$,

which equals 5^{-7}.

> **Guidepost** The meaning behind multiplying numbers with negative exponents.

Here's the second question. *What is $\sqrt[3]{-8}$, or $(-8)^{1/3}$, equal to?* This asks what number, multiplied by itself 3 times, equals -8. Because 3 is an odd number, we can do this. $(-2) \cdot (-2)$ is equal to +4, because a negative times a negative equals a positive. To remind you of why this is true, remember that a negative sign means "take the opposite of." $2 \cdot (-2)$ means move to the left on the number line two places and then two more places. That leaves us at -4. That extra minus sign left over then tells us to take the opposite of this result, meaning we end up at +4. Continuing on, multiply this +4 by another -2, and you have -8. Therefore, $(-2) \cdot (-2) \cdot (-2)$ equals -8, and $\sqrt[3]{-8}$, or $(-8)^{1/3}$, is equal to -2.

Check out Figure 4.13.

Figure 4.13

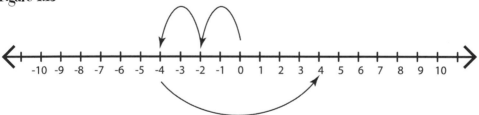

2 · (-2) puts you at (-4). Because it's (-2) · (-2), we take the opposite of 2 · (-2) and end up at (+4).

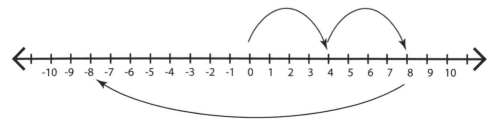

Multiplying 4 by 2 puts you at 8. Because you are multiplying by (-2) rather than 2, you end up at (-8).

Here's the third question. *What is* $\sqrt{16}$ *if you allow negative answers?* We're asking what number multiplied by itself gives you 16. There are two answers. The obvious one is 4, and the not-so-obvious one is -4, because (-4) · (-4) = 16. When you allow negative answers, then the symbol $\sqrt{}$ stands for the **square root** of a number. So, the radical of 16 is equal to 4, and the square root of 16 is equal to either +4 or -4. Now, the question is, how do you know whether $\sqrt{}$ means square root (both positive and negative answers) or radical (just the positive answer)? The answer is that you don't always know, because a number of texts, especially science texts, don't make this distinction. All I can say is that I'll do my best to make the distinction throughout this book, and I'll discuss potential confusion whenever it appears.

Guidepost The difference between square roots and radicals.

Finally, I asked you what $\sqrt{-1}$ is equal to. What number multiplied by itself is equal to -1? For that matter, what number multiplied by itself ever equals a negative number? The answer is that there is no such number, at least not in the sense that we usually think of numbers on a number line. If you multiply a positive number by itself, you get a positive number. If you multiply a negative number by itself, you also get a positive number. Not to be deterred by this annoying fact, mathematicians and scientists have invented an answer to this.[*] The square root of -1 is equal to the number *i*. The number *i* is what is known as an **imaginary number**, and any number multiplied by *i* is also an imaginary number. Seems pretty goofy, huh? I'm not going to deal much with imaginary numbers in this book, but they are extremely useful. Many physical constructs can be represented as having a *real* part and an *imaginary* part, and both parts can be quite useful in figuring out how physical systems work.[9] One example is light waves and their interactions. When you represent a light wave as having both real and imaginary parts, the mathematics of its interactions with other light waves is much easier to do, and actually reveals extra information about those interactions. As I said, I won't be delving into imaginary numbers here, but I wanted you to at least know what *i* in expressions like e^{ix} represents if you come across it in higher math.

---

[*] If you are bothered by the fact that mathematicians can just "invent" a new kind of number, keep in mind that all of mathematics is a human construct. I often state that all of math and science is "made up." Despite the criticism I sometimes get by stating this, I'm sticking with it.

---

[9] A number that contains both a real part and an imaginary part is called a **complex number**.

"Why can't he have imaginary friends like other kids instead of imaginary numbers?!!"

Even more things to do before you read even more explanation

Lookk at the following series of calculations. Try to figure out the pattern and fill in the question marks in the last line.

$$4^5 = 4 \cdot 4 \cdot 4 \cdot 4 \cdot 4$$

$$\frac{4^5}{4^1} = \frac{4 \cdot 4 \cdot 4 \cdot 4 \cdot \not{4}}{\not{4}} = 4^4 = 256$$

$$\frac{4^4}{4^1} = \frac{4 \cdot 4 \cdot 4 \cdot \not{4}}{\not{4}} = 4^3 = 64$$

$$\frac{4^3}{4^1} = \frac{4 \cdot 4 \cdot \not{4}}{\not{4}} = 4^2 = 16$$

$$\frac{4^2}{4^1} = \frac{4 \cdot \not{4}}{\not{4}} = 4^1 = 4$$

$$\frac{4^1}{4^1} = \frac{\not{4}}{\not{4}} = 4^? = ?$$

Even more explanation

Did you figure out the pattern? It's not too difficult if you just look at what is happening to the numbers. The term after the second equals sign in each case goes from 4^4 to 4^3 to 4^2 to 4^1. Using our number line, the next exponent should be 0, right? Therefore, we can replace the last line (with the question marks) with

$$\frac{4^1}{4^1} = \frac{\cancel{4}}{\cancel{4}} = 4^0 = 1$$

This tells us that $4^0 = 1$. In fact, since we can repeat this pattern with any number, not just the number 4, we arrive at the meaning of any number raised to the 0 power. It's just equal to 1.

What does this have to do with negative numbers? To find out, let's continue the pattern. If we keep moving to the left on the number line (our exponents go from 4 to 3 to 2 to 1 to 0), then we arrive at -1 and then -2. Therefore, our pattern looks like this:

$$\frac{4^3}{4^1} = \frac{4 \cdot 4 \cdot \cancel{4}}{\cancel{4}} = 4^2 = 16$$

$$\frac{4^2}{4^1} = \frac{4 \cdot \cancel{4}}{\cancel{4}} = 4^1 = 4$$

$$\frac{4^1}{4^1} = \frac{\cancel{4}}{\cancel{4}} = 4^0 = 1$$

$$\frac{4^0}{4^1} = \frac{1}{4} = 4^{-1} = \frac{1}{4}$$

In the previous chapter, I told you I would justify that a number with a negative exponent is just the reciprocal of the number to the positive exponent, and here's the justification. We can continue the pattern further and state that

$$4^{-1} = \frac{1}{4^1}$$

$$4^{-2} = \frac{1}{4^2}$$

$$4^{-3} = \frac{1}{4^3}$$

and so on.

Chapter Summary

- To properly describe all of the physical occurrences in the world, we need to use both positive and negative numbers.

- Number lines help us represent both positive and negative numbers, and the mathematical interactions among those numbers.

- Subtraction is the same as "adding the opposite." There's a reason for that.

- A positive times a negative equals a negative, and a negative times a negative equals a positive. These rules make perfect sense when you interpret them using a number line.

- A number added to its additive inverse (the negative of the number) is equal to zero. This also makes perfect sense when you interpret it using a number line.

- Taking the square root of a number results in two possible answers—a positive answer and a negative answer. Taking the radical of a number results in just the positive square root of the number.

- The square root of a negative number is not on a number line, but the concept is so useful in science that we define the square root of -1 as the letter *i*. The number *i* is an imaginary number, and anything multiplied by *i* is also an imaginary number.

Applications

1. Remember the commutative property from Chapter 1? We learned there that, for example, 3 + 8 = 8 + 3. That works for addition, but not subtraction. 3 – 8 is not equal to 8 – 3. If we rewrite subtraction as "plus the opposite," though, we can still use the commutative property. 3 – 8 is equal to 3 + (-8), and it *is* true that 3 + (-8) is equal to (-8) + 3. Do the addition if you don't believe me (use the number line!). The key here is that we're using parentheses to keep the minus sign with the 8 as we reverse the order.

2. We've dealt with multiplying negative numbers together and multiplying negative numbers and positive numbers. What about division? We can think physically about dividing a negative number by a positive number, as in $\frac{-6}{2}$. This tells us to divide -6 into two equal pieces. Since it's a *negative* 6, those two equal pieces will be of size -3. $\frac{-6}{-2}$ is a different matter. What does it mean to divide a number into *negative* pieces? That's difficult to picture, but we can rely on our notion that negative means "take the opposite." If $\frac{-6}{2}$ is equal to -3, then the opposite of that result is 3. Of course, we can also rely on the fact that -6 is equal to $(-1) \cdot (6)$ and that -2 is equal to $(-1) \cdot (2)$. Then we can write $\frac{-6}{-2}$ as $\frac{(-1) \cdot (6)}{(-1) \cdot (2)}$. Because $\frac{-1}{-1}$ is equal to 1 (anything divided by itself is equal to 1), we're left with $\frac{6}{2}$, which is equal to 3. And

this leads to the rule that a negative divided by a negative equals a positive while a negative divided by a positive equals a negative. Similarly, a positive divided by a negative equals a negative.

3. Here's a situation that often confuses people. How do you evaluate the expression -3^2? How do you evaluate $(-3)^2$? Are these the same? Answer: No. PEMDAS to the rescue. Parentheses take precedence over all other operations. Exponents are next, and addition and subtraction are last, on equal footing. So, how do we evaluate -3^2? Exponents before subtraction, so -3^2 is equal to -9. With $(-3)^2$, the parentheses take precedence, so this is equal to $(-3) \cdot (-3)$, which equals 9.

4. One thing I haven't covered is division of exponents that have the same base. We know how to evaluate $4^2 \cdot 4^5$, but not $\frac{4^2}{4^5}$. Actually, we have all the understanding necessary to evaluate this, so why not use that understanding instead of just providing a new rule? $\frac{4^2}{4^5}$ is equal to $\frac{4^2}{1} \cdot \frac{1}{4^5}$. I hope you see why. Because $\frac{4^2}{1}$ equals 4^2 and $\frac{1}{4^5}$ equals 4^{-5}, we end up with $\frac{4^2}{4^5}$ being equal to $4^2 \cdot 4^{-5}$. Now we just use the usual "add the exponents" rule and get $4^2 \cdot 4^{-5} = 4^{(2+(-5))} = 4^{-3}$. This is the same result we would get if we simply *subtracted* the bottom exponent from the top exponent in the original division. That provides us with a rule for dealing with division of exponents. When you divide exponents that have the same base, you subtract the bottom exponent from the top exponent.[*] Nothing new, really. Just an extension of our procedure for dealing with multiplication of exponents with the same base. As a quick test, what do you think $\frac{6^4}{6^{-6}}$ equals? If you get the answer 6^{10}, you have the procedure figured out.

---

[*] Remember that the bases of the two numbers *must* be the same. There's not much you can do with an expression such as $\frac{3^5}{4^3}$.

Why Do They Have to Gum Everything Up With Those Letters?

Often people who are relatively comfortable doing math with numbers completely freak out when **variables** (you know, those letters that take the place of numbers) come into the picture. Things start looking much more abstract and complicated. You don't balance your checkbook with letters, do you? Nah. Numbers are just fine. Why do we need those letters? Wouldn't it be easier to just do without them? In some cases, the answer is yes, it would be easier to do without the letters. In many cases, though, the answer is

TIME		BALL
1:30	To play postseason the Cubs must win 56% of their games. If they win 66% of 82 home games, out of the 80 away games they will need:	3
PITCHER	A. to win 33%	STRIKE
23	B. a miracle	1
	C. opponents to concede after the All-Star Game	
BATTER	D. to win 45%	OUT
10		0

	1	2	3	4	5	6	7	8	9	10	R	H	E
HOME	a	3	0	a	1	0					2^3	10	0
VISITOR	0	0	b	x	1	0					6	7	2

Math Day at the Ballpark

69

no. Things can be much simpler when we deal with letters, as I hope to show you in this chapter. In addition to providing examples of when variables are useful, I'll help you develop general expressions for most of the procedures covered in the first four chapters.

Things to do before you read the explanation

Time to pretend you're Galileo. Back in the 1600s, he studied the motion of objects, in particular how objects responded to the pull of gravity. He used ramps to slow things down, but let's pretend he didn't and just watched things fall to the ground. That's what we'll do, or pretend to do. Let's say you dropped a bowling ball from various heights and got the following results.

Height of drop	Time for fall
5 meters	1 second
10 meters	1.41 seconds
15 meters	1.73 seconds
20 meters	2 seconds

Given this data, predict how long it will take for the bowling ball to fall 35 meters. Not obvious, is it?

The explanation

Just by looking at the pattern of heights and times of fall, you might be able to make a pretty good guess as to how long it would take the bowling ball to fall 35 meters. If you graphed the data, you might even get a better answer. But what if you want an exact answer? How can you get that without actually dropping the ball from 35 meters? Well, it turns out that Galileo figured out an exact relationship that allows you to predict how long it will take a bowling ball (chances are he didn't use a bowling ball) to fall a given distance. That relationship is as follows:

$$\text{time for fall} = \sqrt{\frac{2 \cdot \text{distance}}{10}}$$

> **Guidepost** Illustrating the usefulness of variables that represent numbers.

This is a bit of fudge, because the number 10 really should be 9.8. This fudge of substituting 10 for a more accurate number is just to make the calculations easier. That was more important in the days of slide rules, but I guess I'm just a creature of habit. Also, I'm omitting necessary units, but that's not important right now. What I'm going to do is use letters to represent the time and the distance, namely t for the time and d for the distance.

Then the relationship is $t = \sqrt{\frac{2 \cdot d}{10}}$

And just to get you used to the way most relationships are written, I'm going to eliminate that multiplication sign between the 2 and the *d*. Whenever there is a number right next to a letter, or when there are two letters right next to each other, that means you multiply them.[*] So, the relationship becomes[†]

$$t=\sqrt{\frac{2d}{10}}$$

Now we have something powerful. We can figure out how long (*t*) it will take a ball dropped from a height (*d*) to land on the ground. We can know it exactly. So you can put in 35 meters or 50 meters or 2,094 meters, and know how long it will take to fall.[‡] Just for kicks, let's figure out how long it should take our bowling ball to fall 35 meters. All we have to do is substitute the number 35 in for the variable *d*. So, we get

$$t=\sqrt{\frac{2(35)}{10}}$$

$$t=\sqrt{\frac{70}{10}}$$

$$t=\sqrt{7}$$

$$t = 2.6 \text{ seconds}$$

So now we have one great reason for using letters instead of numbers. We can describe general relationships without having to resort to specific numbers.

"You know, Galileo, years from now, on late night TV, they'll drop stuff off buildings just for laughs."

---

[*] This is a common convention in math. A number and a variable right next to each other implies multiplication, as does a variable next to a variable, as do two quantities enclosed in parentheses next to each other. So, all of the following are multiplications: *xy*, 4*b*, and (2+*y*)(*x*+*z*).

[†] If you like reducing fractions to their lowest terms, you might be wondering why I'm using $\sqrt{\frac{2d}{10}}$ instead of $\sqrt{\frac{d}{5}}$. I'm just being faithful to the formula that Galileo, and later Newton, used for this calculation. Call it a physics person's quirk.

[‡] I should mention here one of my favorite quotes from Albert Einstein: "As far as the laws of mathematics refer to reality, they are not certain. As far as they are certain, they do not refer to reality." What that means is that modeling the real world with mathematical relationships almost always ignores a bit of reality. In the case of falling objects, our relationship presented here ignores air friction and the size and weight of the ball that's dropping. Those things are important, and will affect the real answer.

More things to do before you read more explanation

I told you in the introduction to this chapter that you could develop general expressions for all the procedures we've done in the previous four chapters. Let's try that, starting with the calculation of $5^3 \cdot 5^7$. We already know that this is equal to 5^{10}, but can you show that it is true for any base and any exponent? To get you started, I'll provide the general expression, which is $a^m a^n = a^{(m+n)}$. Here the letter a represents the base number, and m and n represent the different exponents.

Now that you've solved that problem, or maybe not, here are a few more challenges. In meeting these challenges, you are going to have to use letters to represent numbers. The idea is that when you use a letter, you can substitute any number for that letter and have the expression make sense.

- Give a general expression that states that any number divided by itself is equal to 1.

- Provide a general expression that states that any number added to its opposite is equal to 0.

- Provide a general expression that states that any number multiplied by its reciprocal is equal to 1. If you forget what a reciprocal is, refer back to Chapters 2 and 3.

Okay, stop. You know I'm going to give you the answers to these challenges in the next section. For real learning, take a moment and try these things for yourself before you look at my answers, OK?

More explanation

I asked you to justify the expression $a^m a^n = a^{(m+n)}$. Here the letter a represents the base, and m and n represent exponents. All these letters are just placeholders for numbers. The point we're trying to make is that this kind of relationship holds true no matter what numbers you put in for a, m, and n. The expression a^m tells us to multiply a by itself m times. The expression a^n tells us to multiply a by itself n times. Therefore, we can represent $a^m a^n$ as in Figure 5.1.

> **Guidepost** Using variables to make general statements about the properties of numbers, in particular exponents.

Because there are m number of a's in the first group and n number of a's in the second group, there is a total of $m + n$ number of a's in all. Therefore, $a^m a^n = a^{(m+n)}$. This is also clear in Figure 5.1.

Figure 5.1

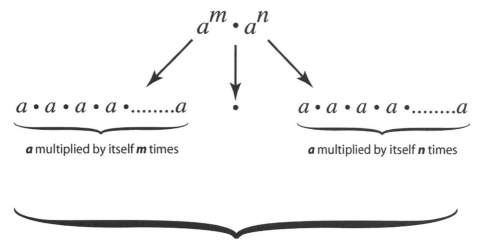

$$a^m \cdot a^n$$

$$a \cdot a \cdot a \cdot a \cdot \ldots\ldots a \qquad \cdot \qquad a \cdot a \cdot a \cdot a \cdot \ldots\ldots a$$

a multiplied by itself ***m*** times   *a* multiplied by itself ***n*** times

a is multiplied a total of ***m + n*** times

So, we've proved this relationship for any set of numbers you want. No matter what you put in for *a*, *m*, and *n*, it will work out.

On to the other challenges.

- *Give a general expression that states that any number divided by itself is equal to 1.* First we have to represent "any number." We can use a variable for that. We could use *a*, *b*, *c*, *x*, *y*, *z*, or any other letter to represent the variable. Just for consistency, let's use *a*. If *a* represents our number, then that same number should also be represented by *a*. Then, "a number divided by itself" is just $\frac{a}{a}$. Now all we have to do is state that this is always equal to 1, as in $\frac{a}{a}$ = 1. Easy, huh? We do need to add one thing, though. Because division by zero is undefined, we have to say that $\frac{a}{a}$ = 1 for *a* $\neq$ 0. Here it helps to know that the symbol $\neq$ means "not equal to."

- *Provide a general expression that states that any number added to its opposite is equal to 0.* This one isn't much more difficult than the previous one, but it's potentially confusing. Once again, we need a letter to represent "any number." Just for kicks, let's use the letter *c*, although we could use *a* again with no trouble. If *c* is the number, then how do we write the opposite of *c*? Just put a negative sign in front of it, as in *-c*. Adding this unspecified number and its opposite means we write the following expression: *c + -c*. Because a number plus its negative equals zero, we can write *c + -c = 0*, and that's the general expression we're looking for. Now that we have that expression, let's address the potential confusion. What does *c* or *–c* mean if the number we're talking about happens to be negative itself? Don't we have to worry about that ahead of time? The answer is no. To see that, let's suppose our letter c represents the number -2. Then we have

$$c + \text{-}c = (\text{-}2) + \text{-}(\text{-}2)$$

> **Guidepost** More use of variables to represent general properties of numbers.

Because the opposite of a negative is a positive, -(-2) is equal to +2, and our expression becomes

$$c + \text{-}c = (\text{-}2) + \text{-}(\text{-}2)$$
$$= \text{-}2 + 2$$

which is equal to zero. This brings up an idea that I'll revisit from time to time, which is that whenever you have letters representing variables, you treat those variables as if they're positive numbers in all calculations. Never worry about what might eventually be substituted for those variables, as that will all come out in the wash.

● *Provide a general expression that states that any number multiplied by its reciprocal is equal to 1. If you forget what a reciprocal is, it's the fractional inverse of a number.* Once again, we need a letter to represent "any number." Let's go back to using a. If a is our number, then the reciprocal of a is $\frac{1}{a}$, just as if 6 is the number, then its reciprocal is $\frac{1}{6}$. So, a number multiplied by its reciprocal looks like $a \cdot \frac{1}{a}$. If we want to say that this expression is equal to 1, then we write

$$a \cdot \frac{1}{a} = 1 \text{ for } a \neq 0$$

Just to illustrate that we can use variables in the same way that we use numbers, let's rewrite a as $\frac{a}{1}$, so our expression becomes $\frac{a}{1} \cdot \frac{1}{a} = 1$. Now we just use our rule for multiplying fractions, which is that you multiply the numerators and multiply the denominators. $\frac{a}{1} \cdot \frac{1}{a} = \frac{a \cdot 1}{1 \cdot a}$, which is equal to $\frac{a}{a}$, which is equal to 1. As always, division by zero is a no-no, so we should also specify that a cannot equal 0.

Even more things to do before you read even more explanation

Time for some basic math operations involving variables and numbers. I'll give you challenges that go from simple to complex. In each expression that follows, treat each variable as if it always stands for the same thing. For example, in the expression $x + 3z - 4x + a$, the x's stand for the same quantity even though we don't know what number x represents. The z and a stand for numbers other than the one x represents. Okay, here are the challenges.

- What does $x + x$ equal? How about $4x + 2x$?

- Try mixing numbers and variables. What does $3x + 2$ equal?

- More variables and numbers. See if you can write an equivalent expression for $(4qr)^3$.

- Time to get really complicated. See if you can simplify the following expression. $6x^2 - 3x + 2q - x^2 + y^2 - q + q^3 + 4(x + y)$.

Even more explanation

If the very first challenge made beads of sweat form on your forehead, then you officially have variable-phobia. Many who suffer from that sickness object to the very idea of adding things together when they don't even know what numbers those letters stand for. It's really not a problem, though. The expression is $x + x$. If I told you that x was equal to 5, you wouldn't have a problem. $x + x$ would just equal $5 + 5$. Of course, I haven't told you that x is equal to 5, so we have to take a different route. If I add one x to a second x, how many x's do I have? Yep, two x's. Therefore, $x + x$ is just equal to $2x$. And that's true for any number you put in for x. If x is equal to 5, then two x's equal two 5s, which is equal to 10, which is what you would get if you added $5 + 5$. So, we can add those variables even if we don't know what number or numbers they represent. The key is that we're adding **like terms**. Each x represents the same number, whatever that number is.

Like terms and unlike terms. Suppose you have two kinds of boxes, one painted red and one painted blue. All red boxes have the same contents and all blue boxes have the same contents, but the contents of the red boxes are different from the contents of the blue boxes. Now, suppose there are two collections of red boxes. There are 4 red boxes in one group and 7 red boxes in the other group. Can you combine these two groups and say you have 11 red boxes altogether? Of course you can.

Next, suppose you have 4 red boxes in one group and 7 blue boxes in another group. Can you combine these two groups and say you have 11 red-blue boxes altogether? Not really, because the contents of the boxes are different. The simplest way to describe the situation is to say that you have 4 red boxes and 11 blue boxes.

When you have two groups of red boxes, you have "like boxes," and you can combine them. When you have one group of red boxes and one group of blue boxes, you have "unlike boxes," and you can't combine them in any meaningful way. The situation with variables is the same as with the boxes. If you have an expression like $x + x$, or an expression like $4x + 2x$, each x represents the same number or numbers. We can combine the x's in each case and end up with $2x$ and $6x$. If, however, we have an expression like $x + y$, the x and y represent different things, just as the red and blue boxes represent different things. We call x and y "unlike" terms, and we can't combine them in any meaningful way.

Now that we know that $x + x = 2x$, $4x + 2x$ is pretty easy. It's just equal to $6x$. To convince yourself this is true, just put in any number you want for x, and $4x + 2x = 6x$ is a true statement.

On to $3x + 2$. A common mistake people make is to combine these terms, saying that $3x + 2$ is the same as $5x$, or that $3x + 2$ is the same as 5. The reason that's a mistake is that we don't know what x represents, and until we do, we can't go around adding x to a definite number. It's similar to the situation in the previous text box, where the x represents a red box and the 2 is a different-color box. If x represents the number 2, then $3x + 2$ is equal to 8. If x represents the number 3, then $3x + 2$ is equal to 11. So, there is no way to simplify $3x + 2$. It is what it is. The rule is that you can combine like terms and that you *cannot* combine **unlike terms**. The reason behind the rule in this case is that you can't add a number to a variable (at least not and get a definite answer) until you know what the variable represents.

Guidepost Rules for combining terms in a math expression.

Our next challenge is to write a new expression for $(4qr)^*$. Well, that expression is fine as is. All we need to do is multiply 4 by q and then by r, and cube the result.[4] We can write an equivalent expression, though. Remember that variables follow the same rules as positive numbers. Therefore, $(4qr)^3$ is equal to $4^3 \cdot q^3 \cdot r^3$. How do we know that? We can just use the rule for raising a product of numbers to a power, or we can write it out as follows: $(4qr)^3$ equals $(4qr) \cdot (4qr) \cdot (4qr)$. Because we can change the order and grouping when multiplying things (commutative and associative properties), this expression is just equal to $(4 \cdot 4 \cdot 4) \cdot (q \cdot q \cdot q) \cdot (r \cdot r \cdot r)$, which is equal to $4^3 \cdot q^3 \cdot r^3$.

The last expression in the previous "things to do" section looks the scariest. How can you simplify $6x^2 - 3x + 2q - x^2 + y^2 - q + q^3 + 4(x + y)$? It's actually not so bad if you keep in mind what the letters, numbers, and symbols represent. For starters, we *can't* combine a q with an x, because although each q and each x represent a given number, those two variables do not represent the *same* number. You can't add x and q to get two of anything, because you don't know ahead of time what those letters represent. Think back to the red and blue boxes. Similarly, we can't add x to x^2 until we know what x represents. For example, suppose x is equal to 3. Then $x + x^2$ is equal to $3 + 9$, which is equal to 12. If x is equal to 4, though, then $x + x^2$ is equal to $4 + 16$, which is equal to 20. Because a number and the square of the number are different, x and x^2 are like red and blue boxes—they have different contents. There is no simpler way to write $x + x^2$ than as $x + x^2$. Once again, we can't combine unlike terms.

---

[*] "Cubing" something means you raise it to the third power, or multiply it by itself three times.

Okay, on to simplifying our expression. The first thing I'm going to do is transform every subtraction into "plus a negative." The reason for doing that is that once we have all additions and no subtractions, then we can change the order all we want with no trouble.

$$6x^2 - 3x + 2q - x^2 + y^2 - q + q^3 + 4(x + y)$$

then becomes

$$6x^2 + (-3x) + 2q + (-x^2) + y^2 + (-q) + q^3 + 4(x + y).$$

The next thing that might cause a little trouble is that last term, $4(x + y)$. Easy to solve that problem, though. We just use the distributive property[*] and find that $4(x + y)$ is equal to $4x + 4y$. Now the full expression is

$$6x^2 + (-3x) + 2q + (-x^2) + y^2 + (-q) + q^3 + 4x + 4y.$$

Now I'm going to arrange this expression so that "like terms" are together.

$$6x^2 + (-x^2) + 4x + (-3x) + 2q + (-q) + y^2 + q^3 + 4y$$

And now that the like terms are together, I'll combine the like terms. $6x^2 + (-x^2)$ is equal to $5x^2$, $4x + (-3x)$ is equal to x, and $2q + (-q)$ is equal to q. We're left with

$$5x^2 + x + q + y^2 + q^3 + 4y.$$

That's as far as we can go, because we can't combine terms that have different exponents and we can't combine different variables. Often, just to make things look nice, people will put all the x, y, and q terms next to one another, as in

$$5x^2 + x + q^3 + q + y^2 + 4y,$$

but that's not absolutely necessary.

If you've done and/or taught much algebra, the steps I just went through shouldn't be too foreign. As you do problems of this type, the procedure becomes somewhat automatic, and that's fine. My only suggestion is that, if you ever get slightly confused about the procedures, slow down and make sure each step makes sense to you. You should ultimately know why you can combine some terms and not others. And with that, I'm not going to cover anything else with variables except to provide more examples in the Applications section of this chapter. Keep in mind that my goal is to help you *understand* the procedures rather than become proficient at *doing* them. Once you understand, simple practice will take care of the "doing" part.

---

[*] Refer back to Chapter 1 for a review of the distributive property.

Chapter Summary

- Variables are letters that serve as placeholders for numbers.

- We can use variables to represent mathematical relationships between physical quantities.

- We can use variables to express general properties of numbers, such as

$$a^m a^n = a^{(m+n)}, \; a \cdot \frac{1}{a} = 1, \text{ and } a + (-a) = 0.$$

- To simplify math expressions, you can combine like terms but cannot combine unlike terms. Like terms are those that contain identical variables with identical exponents. x^2, $2x^2$, and $-45x^2$ are all like terms, but x^3, $3y$, $-5x$, and $2xy$ are all unlike terms.

Applications

1. There are so many science relationships that use variables, I could fill the rest of the book with them. For now, I'll just address a really common one, which is the famous *distance = rate · time*. The basis for this relationship is the definition of speed,[*] but it's also almost common sense. If you travel at a speed of 10 miles per hour for a period of 3 hours, you've gone 30 miles, right (let's hope you're on a bike instead of in a car)? That's just an application of our relationship, which we can write with variables as

   distance = rate · time

   $d = r \cdot t$

   Putting in our numbers, we get

   $d = r \cdot t$

   $d = (10 \; \frac{\text{miles}}{\text{hour}}) \cdot (3 \text{ hours})$

   $= \left(10 \frac{\text{miles}}{\cancel{\text{hour}}}\right) \cdot (3 \text{ hours}) \text{ hours units cancel}$

   $= 30 \text{ miles}$

   That might seem simple, but suppose you had to rethink how distance, rate, and time are related every time you did a calculation. That would be more than cumbersome. A simple relationship with variables tells us how it works every time. Neat.

---

[*] See the *Stop Faking It!* book on Force and Motion.

2. I covered the relationship $a^m a^n = a^{(m+n)}$ in this chapter. What about $\frac{a^m}{a^n}$? Do we have a general expression for the result when you divide exponents of the same base? Sure. All we have to do is remember that a negative exponent means take the reciprocal of the base to the positive exponent. That means that $\frac{1}{a^n}$ is equal to a^{-n}. Keep in mind that when dealing with variables, you treat them just as if they're positive numbers. Even though we write the exponent here as $-n$, that says nothing about whether n is actually positive or negative. As I said, it all comes out in the wash in the end. Anyway, $\frac{a^m}{a^n}$ is equal to $\frac{a^m}{1} \cdot \frac{1}{a^n}$, which is equal to $a^m \cdot \frac{1}{a^n}$, which is equal to $a^m \cdot a^{-n}$. Because you add the exponents when you multiply terms with the same base, this equals $a^{(m+(-n))}$, which is equal to $a^{(m-n)}$, and we have our general statement. $\frac{a^m}{a^n} = a^{m-n}$. Of course, this isn't complete, because we haven't specified that a cannot equal zero, so a better statement is $\frac{a^m}{a^n} = a^{m-n}$, for $a \neq 0$.

3. Anyone who's ever opened an algebra book knows about the FOIL method for multiplying two sums that are in parentheses, as in $(a + b)(c + d)$. Here I'm using the letters a, b, c, and d to represent any numbers or letters or combinations thereof. FOIL stands for First, Outside, Inside, Last. Figure 5.2 shows how to apply it to get the result $(a + b)(c + d) = ac + ad + bc + bd$.

Figure 5.2

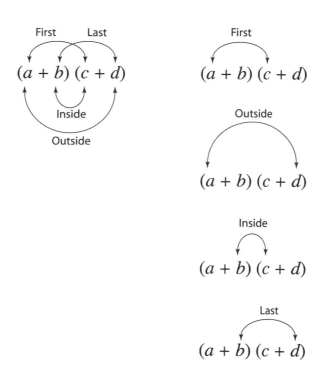

The FOIL method, although a useful memory tool, is really nothing more than repeated application of the distributive property. To see that, let's treat the expression $(a + b)$ as a single expression. Then $(a + b)(c + d)$ is equal to $(a + b) \cdot c + (a + b) \cdot d$. Now I'm going to do something just a bit different from how I've done it in the past. I'm going to use the distributive property even though the terms multiplying the parentheses are on the right instead of the left.* $(a + b) \cdot c$ is equal to $a \cdot c + b \cdot c$, and $(a + b) \cdot d$ is equal to $a \cdot d + b \cdot d$. Okay, we started with $(a + b)(c + d)$. We used the distributive property to get $(a + b) \cdot c + (a + b) \cdot d$. Then we used the distributive property again to end up with $a \cdot c + b \cdot c + a \cdot d + b \cdot d$. All we have to do is rearrange the order of addition (we can do that because of the commutative property) and get $a \cdot c + a \cdot d + b \cdot c + b \cdot d$. First, outside, inside, last. Yes, a rule, but a rule that makes sense.†

"Curses! FOIL-ed again!"

---

* We can do this because multiplication is commutative, meaning that order doesn't matter in multiplication.

---

† Maybe you're getting tired of me harping on this idea of things making sense. If it's any consolation, I'm beginning to make fun of myself every time I mention it. I keep thinking of the movie *The Miracle Worker*, in which Anne Bancroft keeps saying, "Water, it has a name.... Tree, it has a name.... A math rule, it makes sense." No, Anne didn't say that last one.

Ack! Word Problems!

One of my favorite "Far Side" comics involves someone at the Pearly Gates of Heaven. Saint Peter is at the gates and says, "Okay, now listen up. Nobody gets in here without answering the following question: A train leaves Philadelphia at 1:00 PM. It's traveling at 65 miles per hour. Another train leaves Denver at 4:00.... Say, you need a pencil and paper?" The caption under the cartoon is "Math phobic's nightmare." Yep, word problems scare people. They *should* scare you if your method of doing math is to memorize procedures, but they're not all that awful if you take the time to understand what's going on.

Most textbooks go through the procedures for solving math equations before they ever get to word problems, but I think that's a bit backwards. I figure you ought to know where the equations come from in the first place, so you might actually have a reason for solving them. So, solving equations is in the following chapter. Here we're going to try to make sense of the process of creating equations.

Things to do before you read the explanation

One of the "classic" word problems is that of combining various mixtures to come up with a final mixture. You're supposed to figure out how many liters of some mixture need to be combined with so many liters of another mixture to get the final mixture. Try the following activity to help you see what those silly mixture problems are all about.

Get three clear drinking glasses that all have the same uniform diameter, meaning they're straight up and down on the outside (not tapered) and are all of the same width. Identical glasses will do the trick. Then get a bottle of vegetable oil and some masking tape. Fill one of the glasses maybe ¼ full of water. Then pour maybe another ¼ of a glass of vegetable oil on top of the water (you don't have to be exact with the fractions). Do this slowly, preferably against the side of the glass while it's tipped, so the oil and water don't mix very well. The oil should float on top of the water. Next create another layer of vegetable oil on top of water in a second glass. The fractions aren't important, but you should make sure that you don't have so much oil and water combined in the glasses that they'll overflow the third glass when you combine everything. See Figure 6.1.

Figure 6.1

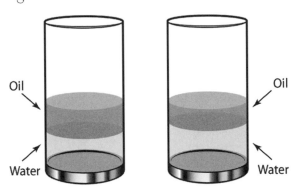

Oil

Water

Oil

Water

Before you combine anything, measure the heights of each liquid in each glass. You can do this by marking the levels with masking tape and then measuring the heights, or simply by measuring the heights directly. See Figure 6.2.

OK, go ahead and pour the contents of your two glasses into the third, empty glass. Even if you do this slowly, the oil and water will mix a bit, so after combining the liquids in the third glass,

Figure 6.2

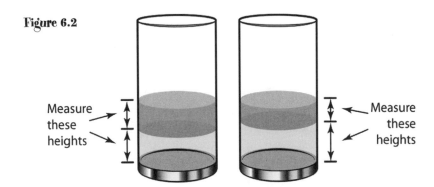

Measure these heights

Measure these heights

wait a while for the oil and water to separate. Once the oil clearly is floating on top of the water in the third glass, measure the heights of each liquid, as in Figure 6.3.

The explanation

I'm going to make the bold assumption that you wrote down those heights of oil in each glass. What you need to do is add the height of the oil in the first glass to the height of the oil in the second glass. Now that you have that answer, compare that number to the height of the oil in the final mixture. Within a centimeter or two, are they the same? Say, "Yes."

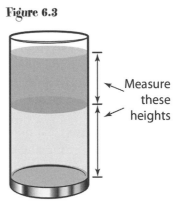

Figure 6.3

Measure these heights

Now for a statement of the obvious. The amount of oil in the first glass plus the amount of oil in the second glass equals the amount of oil in the final glass. Even if oil and water mixed completely, that would be a true statement, which brings us to a general method for solving mixture problems. Here's a typical one. A chemist wants to create a solution that is 15% antifreeze.* She starts with 5 liters of a 25% antifreeze solution. How many liters of 10% solution should she add to this to end up with a 15% solution? Now, when I saw problems like this in high school chemistry, I would try to remember what they did in a similar problem in the textbook. I knew there had to be a couple of x's in there, and I knew I needed to use all the numbers in the problem, and I knew that I had to add an expression involving those numbers and x's to another expression and get some final expression. In other words, I didn't try to think the problem through from scratch. I just tried to write down the proper equation from memory. Sound familiar? Well, there's a better way.

We have three solutions—the 25% solution, the 10% solution we add to it, and the final 15% solution. This is exactly like the oil and water mixtures you did, so we can write a general principle.

(amount of pure antifreeze in the 25% solution) + (amount of pure antifreeze in the 10% solution) = (amount of pure antifreeze in the final 15% solution)

Guidepost Using a word equation as a method for translating a word problem into a math equation.

---

* A 15% solution is 15% pure antifreeze and 85% water. And in case you forgot what % means, it is "per cent" or "per hundred." Therefore, if you have 100 liters of a 15% solution, there are 15 liters of pure antifreeze and 85 liters of water.

I call this a **word equation**, because it expresses something important about the stated problem, and it's expressed as an equation. Believe it or not, this statement will solve our problem for us. We just need to do a bit of translating into math expressions. First, we don't know how much of the 10% solution we need, so we're going to use the variable x to represent that amount.

x = number of liters of 10% solution.

Defining what our variable x represents is the first place people tend to mess up. In teaching algebra, I require students to explain everything they're doing, so a common statement they make is

x = 10% solution

Guidepost Precise definition of variables.

That's just not precise enough, though. Does the variable x stand for the entire solution? Nope. It represents the *number of liters* of the 10% solution. If you start out being vague when defining what your variable represents, you're on the road to confusion, and we all travel that road often enough without doing it intentionally. So, a better definition of x is

x = number of liters of 10% solution

Anyway, the next thing we need to do is begin writing those terms in our word equation as math expressions. Let's start with the second expression, which is (amount of pure antifreeze in the 10% solution). We have x liters of that solution, and 10% of it is pure antifreeze. Let's stop and ask how we can find 10% of anything. What is 10% of 50 cents? Well, 10% when considering money means that for every 100 cents you're dealing with 10 cents (remember, percent means "per hundred"). We can reason this through and decide that if we have 10 cents for every 100 cents, then we have 5 cents for every 50 cents. Therefore, 10% of 50 cents is 5 cents. There's a more general expression, though. In order to find 10% of a number, we just multiply that number by 0.1,[*] giving us one-tenth of the number. Therefore, we get

(amount of pure antifreeze in the 10% solution) =
0.1 · (number of liters of solution) = $0.1x$

Guidepost Moving from a word equation to mathematical expressions.

---

[*] 10% is the same as $\frac{10}{100}$, which is the same as $\frac{1}{10}$, which is the same as 0.1.

Okay, let's tackle the first expression in our word problem, which is (amount of pure antifreeze in the 25% solution). This one is easier than the second expression, because we not only know the percentage of pure antifreeze in the solution, we know how many liters we have of it. Instead of multiplying the number of liters by 0.1, we multiply by 0.25, because we're talking about a 25% solution.

$$\text{(amount of pure antifreeze in the 25\% solution)} =$$
$$0.25 \cdot \text{(number of liters of solution)} = 0.25 \cdot 10$$

We now have two of our expressions. Time to tackle the last one, which is (amount of pure antifreeze in the final 15% solution). Once again, we're just figuring out a percentage.

$$\text{(amount of pure antifreeze in the final 15\% solution)} =$$
$$0.15 \cdot \text{(number of liters of final solution)}$$

We have a snag. Because we don't yet know how many liters of 10% solution we're using (remember, that's what x represents), we don't know how many liters we'll end up with altogether. This isn't a big snag, though. We have 10 liters of the first solution and x liters of the second solution, so we end up with $(10 + x)$ liters in the total. So, we have

$$\text{(amount of pure antifreeze in the final 15\% solution)} =$$
$$0.15 \cdot \text{(number of liters of final solution)} = 0.15 \cdot (10 + x)$$

And we're done. Below are the original word equation and our final equation using math expressions.

(amount of pure antifreeze in the 25% solution) + (amount of pure antifreeze in the 10% solution) = (amount of pure antifreeze in the final 15% solution)

$$0.25 \cdot 10 + 0.1x = 0.15 \cdot (10 + x)$$

We're not completely done, because we still don't know what value of x will make this a true statement. I'll address solving this and other algebraic equations in the next chapter. For now, think about what we did to get to this equation. We started with a physical situation and described that situation with a word equation. We then set about using a variable to represent a quantity we don't know, and then translating each expression in our word equation into a math expression using numbers and that variable. That might seem like a long process, but it beats the heck out of trying to remember what the equation should look like based on a textbook example and then just plunging ahead.

More things to do before you read more explanation

Get a sheet of red construction paper and a sheet of blue construction paper. The actual colors don't matter, but I'll assume you have red and blue just so I can refer to them. Cut each sheet into little squares, making sure you have different numbers of red and blue squares. The squares don't have to be the same size, but you should have about twice as many red as blue squares. No need to count them. Place all your squares in a big bowl and mix them up really well. Then close your eyes and pick 10 squares from the bowl. Count the number of red and blue squares in that 10. Based on your count, estimate the fraction of blue squares and the fraction of red squares in the bowl. If you're a detail person, go ahead and count the total number of red and blue squares in the bowl to see if you're right.

More explanation

What you just did is known as **sampling** a population. You took a small sample of squares and then made a generalization about the fraction of red and blue squares in the entire bowl. Of course, maybe you had trouble figuring out how to estimate the fractions based on your sample. Word problems to the rescue!

If you managed to take a completely random sample of paper pieces from the bowl (probably not all that likely unless you mixed them up for 20 minutes), then you might expect that the sample you took was representative of all of the paper pieces in the bowl. In other words, you would expect to get about the same fraction of blue pieces in your sample as the fraction of all pieces in the bowl that were blue. We can write that as a word equation.

(fraction of blue pieces in the bowl) = (fraction of blue pieces in the sample)

> **Guidepost**   Creating an equation that represents sampling a population.

Keeping in mind that we're estimating here and that the above statement isn't a true equality, let's try to represent those words as math expressions. Since we're after the fraction of blue pieces in the bowl, we can let that entire expression be equal to x.

x = fraction of blue pieces in the bowl

Next we need to clarify the expression on the right with a few more words.

$$\text{Fraction of blue pieces in the sample} = \frac{\text{number of blue pieces in the sample}}{\text{total number of red and blue pieces in the sample}}$$

$$x = \frac{\text{number of blue pieces in the sample}}{\text{total number of red and blue pieces in the sample}}$$

Now it's just a simple matter of putting in numbers for those words on the right. It really is simple because you counted the number of blue pieces in your sample of 10. Let's suppose you got 3 blue pieces out of 10. Then our equation becomes

$$x = \frac{\text{number of blue pieces in the sample}}{\text{total number of red and blue pieces in the sample}} = \frac{3}{10}$$

So we're done. We estimate that the fraction of blue pieces in the bowl is $\frac{3}{10}$.

You might be asking yourself why I chose such a simple problem. The reason is that we use sampling data in many, many places. Every time you see the results of a poll, be it of political views, entertainment preferences, or restaurant choices, that poll is a sampling of the general population. Scientists use samples of animal populations all the time to figure out the habits of those animals. What do you think the business of "tagging animals" is all about? Of course, good sampling procedures involve more than the simple model of pulling pieces of paper out of a bowl. All sorts of things can make a sampling legitimate or illegitimate, but it would take me another chapter to address all of them.

Even more things to do before you read even more explanation

Find a friend and a couple of toy cars or trucks. These toys should roll easily and move more or less in a straight line when you roll them on a smooth surface. You and your friend should kneel down maybe 3 meters apart on a smooth surface, car or truck in hand. Linoleum and concrete work well for the surface. Next you have to coordinate your efforts with your friend's efforts. You are going to send the cars or trucks toward each other at the same time. The instant you release the cars or trucks, you need to count to yourself, determining how many seconds it

Figure 6.4

takes for the cars or trucks to collide. The counting should be your basic, "One one thousand, two one thousand, three one thousand, ..." Of course, if you have a couple of stopwatches, use them. Figure 6.4 shows the procedure.

Try this a couple of times, and compare with your partner how long it took before the collision each time. You might also note who pushed his or her car or truck harder, and where the collision occurred. Was the collision closer to the person who pushed harder, or closer to the person who pushed with less of a force? There's no need to get violent with this activity, but if it makes you feel better, go for it and try to destroy the other toy. I should mention for all the Gomez Adams[*] fans out there that you can do this collision activity with model trains and explosives. Adjust as needed.

Even more explanation

I figured that I ought to explain the kinds of problems addressed with the example of the "Far Side" cartoon referred to at the beginning of this chapter. It's only fair. Hopefully you and your friend found that the "time to collision" for the toys was the same for each toy. That time will change depending on how hard you push the toys, but it is identical for each toy in a given collision. The other thing you might have noticed was that, even though each toy traveled a different distance, the total distance traveled (adding each toy's distance) is the distance between you and your friend. See Figure 6.5.

> **Guidepost** Creating a math equation that represents a simple motion problem.

Figure 6.5

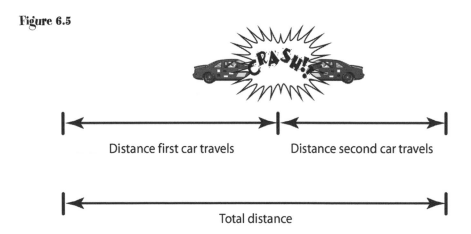

Distance first car travels　　　Distance second car travels

Total distance

---

[*] That would be Gomez Adams from the TV show *The Adams Family*.

This is all the information we need to solve the following problem.

Two trains leave cities that are 50 miles apart, heading toward each other. One travels at 60 miles per hour and the other travels at 40 miles per hour. At what point between the cities do the trains meet? How long before they meet?

We can write word equations for the conditions on the problem. They are

(distance traveled by train 1) + (distance traveled by train 2) = distance between the cities

(time of travel for train 1) = (time of travel for train 2)

We have one other bit of information, which is that for each train, the relationship *distance = rate · time* holds true. I'm going to use subscripts to write this relationship for each train, as in $d_1 = r_1 t_1$ and $d_2 = r_2 t_2$. Now all we have to do is use these relationships in translating the word equations.

So, (distance traveled by train 1) + (distance traveled by train 2) = distance between the cities becomes $d_1 + d_2 = 50$ miles, which we can rewrite as $r_1 t_1 + r_2 t_2 = 50$ miles. We know that r_1 is equal to 40 miles per hour and that r_2 is equal to 60 miles per hour, so the equation now becomes $40 \cdot t_1 + 60 \cdot t_2 = 50$.

In the second equation, (time of travel for train 1) = (time of travel for train 2) becomes $t_1 = t_2$.

These two equations are enough to solve for the time, which we can then use to find the distance traveled by each train. I'll do this solution in the next chapter.

Apparently Car A, traveling at 30 mph., was headed eastbound and Car B, traveling at 38 mph., was headed westbound when they met at 10:33 this morning...

When Life imitates Math

I could fill up the rest of the book with examples of translating word problems into math equations, but I won't. I just wanted to do enough examples to demonstrate that it's possible to set up word problems without memorizing problem types. If you use the information in the problem to create a word equation first, you are well on your way. Then it's a matter of carefully defining your variables (usually these are the "unknowns") and translating that word equation into math expressions.

Chapter Summary

- Translating a word problem into a mathematical equation should be a methodical process rather than a quick, memorized process.

- Developing a word equation is often an important step in the translation of a word problem into a math equation.

- When specifying variables to be used in a word problem, it helps to be precise about what the variables represent.

- You can use fractions to help estimate the numbers in a large population from a relatively small sample.

Applications

1. Here's another mixture problem. *A chemist wants to get a 10% solution of sodium hydroxide. How many liters of a 20% solution should he mix with 5 liters of a 30% solution to get that 10% solution?* Think for a minute how you would solve this problem. Same as the example I did in the chapter, right? Nope. If you take a look at the numbers, you'll realize that you can't solve this problem. There is no way that mixing a 20% solution and a 30% solution will give you a 10% solution because the final solution is less concentrated than the component solutions. The only way to get this lower concentration is to add pure water to one of the other solutions. Posing unsolvable problems is one way to determine whether someone is thinking about the physical situation or memorizing procedures. For all you chemistry teachers out there, try putting this problem on an exam. My bet is that at least half the students will dutifully write down an equation and try to solve it!

2. And yet another mixture problem. How much water must you mix with 2 liters of a 25% antifreeze solution to get a solution that is 10% antifreeze? Clearly this is doable, because a 10% solution is less concentrated than the original 25% solution. This is not exactly like the example in the chapter, though, so it does require more than simply following a memorized procedure. Our word equation still applies, and it's

(amount of pure antifreeze in the 25% solution) + (amount of pure antifreeze in the water) = (amount of pure antifreeze in the final 10% solution)

We don't know how much water to add, so let x equal the number of liters of added water. We have 2 liters of the original solution, so the first term in our word equation is just like the example in the chapter: (amount of pure antifreeze in the 25% solution) is equal to $0.25 \cdot$ (number of liters of 25% solution) = $0.25 \cdot 2$. Now on to the second term in our word equation. How do we express the amount of pure antifreeze in water as a math expression? The answer is simple if you think about it. There isn't any antifreeze in pure water, so the second term is equal to zero! This is where you might get hung up if you memorize procedures. Because the example in the chapter had a second term on the left side, you might be tempted to put in some percentage times x for that term. But the term is zero, so you just move on. The term on the right is similar to the example in the chapter. There are $2 + x$ liters of the final solution, so the amount of pure antifreeze in the final solution is $0.10 \cdot (2 + x)$. Then the final equation is

$$0.25 \cdot (2) + 0 = 0.10 \cdot (2 + x).$$

For the record, a problem that looks different on the surface from previous examples, yet requires the same concepts for solution, is referred to as a **transfer problem**. Using transfer problems on exams is a good way to test whether or not the students really understand concepts.

3. Another common word problem in textbooks asks students to figure out how someone should distribute a given amount of money in two interest-bearing accounts to end up with a certain amount of total interest earned. Here's a typical problem. *Betty invests a total of $2,000 in two savings accounts. One earns 4% simple interest and the other earns 2% simple interest. At the end of the year, she has earned a total of $50. How much did she invest in each account?* I'll give you the proper word equation and definition of variables and let you take it from there. The word equation is

(interest earned on the 4% account) + (interest earned on the 2% account) = 50 dollars

Because we don't know how much was invested in each account, we can let x represent one of those amounts.

x = amount of money invested at 4%

Notice that this is a specific statement. The variable x is not equal to 4%, nor is it equal to the 4% account. It's the *amount of money* invested at 4%. Now, since the total invested is $2,000, the amount of money invested in the 2% account is $(2,000 - x)$. Okay, you're all set. Just translate the word equation into math expressions involving x.

4. If you've ever watched poker tournaments on television, then you know that next to the display of someone's cards, they show the chance of that person winning the hand, expressed as a percentage. How do they get those numbers? It's really no different from the activity where I had you choose red and blue pieces of paper from a bowl. Because there is a definite fraction of blue and red pieces in the bowl, you can make an assumption about what fraction you'll get in a sample. A deck of cards has a definite number of hearts, spades, diamonds, and clubs, along with a definite number of each card within a suit. When you draw a poker hand from a deck of cards, you are taking a sample from the deck. Based on the number and kind of cards in the deck, you can determine the probability of getting any one poker hand. In fact, that probability is what determines the rank of poker hands in the first place. On top of that, your chance of getting a given card depends on what cards have already been dealt. For example, if four jacks have already been dealt, your chance of drawing a jack is zero! I'm not going to pretend that the actual calculation of probabilities is simple, because you have to consider what cards are already in someone's hand, what cards have been dealt, and what the original fractions are. I'm sure they use a computer program to come up with those percentages on television. The basic idea, though, is relatively simple.

5. Even simpler than poker is the game of blackjack. It's simple enough, in fact, that people can "count cards" and determine when their chance of winning is greater or less depending on the cards that have been dealt. If many face cards have already been dealt, then you know that the majority of cards left in the deck are not face cards, and you have a better chance of not going over 21 when you hit your hand. Of course, these are only probabilities. Even if there is only one face card left in the deck, Murphy's law could dictate that you will get that card just when you don't need it. By the way, most casinos now deal blackjack from a "shoe" that contains maybe four decks of cards, making counting the cards much more difficult.

All Things Being Equal ...
Or Not

Now that we've covered at least a few examples of how we get equations from the physical world, it's time to work on solving those equations. Solving an equation means figuring out what values of the unknowns (the variables) will make the equality a true statement. Sometimes there is only one solution, and sometimes there are a number of solutions. How exciting to have different possibilities, eh? Speaking of different possibilities, sometimes the real world gives us relationships that are **inequalities**. I'll introduce those in this chapter and we'll learn how to solve them.

Things to do before you read the explanation

I try to limit the materials you need for activities in this book to things you have around the house or can obtain easily. Gotta make an exception here, though. Try to get your hands on a double-pan balance, illustrated in Figure 7.1. This doesn't have to be an expensive one. They make plastic balances that are pretty inexpensive and are often included in kits that come with elementary-level math and science curricula. Make sure what you have is a double-pan balance and not a triple-beam balance, which is also illustrated in Figure 7.1.

Figure 7.1

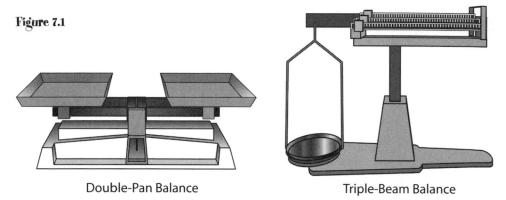

Double-Pan Balance   Triple-Beam Balance

In addition to the balance, you'll need maybe 25 small objects that all have the same weight. If you have access to those math and science kits, then you'll undoubtedly find a bunch of small cubes of the same size or short rods of the same size. You could also go to the hardware store and get a bunch of small nuts (the kind that go on screws, not the kind hanging out in front of the store) or washers that are all the same size. Pennies will also work, and since washers and nuts cost more than a penny each, pennies are the economical route.

Place five nuts* on one side of the balance and five nuts on the other side. Things should be in balance. Then add three nuts to one side and three nuts to the other. Still in balance, yes? Try adding three nuts to one side and only two to the other. Not in balance, right?

With things in balance, remove a couple of nuts from one side and a couple of nuts from the other side. Still in balance? Now for something completely different.† Take one nut from one side, move it to the other side, and somehow make it have the opposite effect on the new side that it had on the previous side. Don't look at me—I have absolutely no idea how you're going to do that!

---

* Of course you could be using cubes or washers or pennies or something else, but it's more fun for me to call them nuts!

---

† All due credit to Monty Python.

Start with three nuts on each side of the balance and then multiply the number on each side by four, meaning you end up with 12 on each side. Then divide each side (they now have 12 on each side) by 4. What do you end up with on each side? Still in balance? Yep.

The explanation

Those basic things I had you do demonstrate one fact about balances.

Things will stay in balance as long as you do exactly the same thing to both sides.

You can add, subtract, multiply, and divide the contents on each side of a balance, and as long as it's the same operation, the balance will stay in balance. Not an astounding revelation, I know.

More not-so-astounding concepts: Suppose you have two basketball teams that are evenly matched. Every time these two teams play it's a tie, even after 10 overtimes. Now suppose you add Lisa Leslie to one team and her clone to the other team.[*] Would they still be evenly matched? Sure. Suppose the best player on one of the teams tears an ACL[†] and the best player on the other team, who happens to be equal in ability to the best player on the first team, also tears an ACL. That amounts to subtracting equal players from each team. The teams are

---

[*] For those who don't know, Lisa Leslie is a big, bad basketball player in the WNBA.

[†] ACL stands for anterior cruciate ligament—a tear to the ACL is a common sports injury.

still equal. I could go on and on, with analogies for multiplying and dividing with basketball teams, but I'm guessing you get the idea, and it's time to move on to math equations.

Below is a math equation to solve. You're supposed to figure out what you can substitute for the variable y so you end up with a true statement. Of course, we're going to assume that this equation came from a real-world situation and that you are truly interested in the answer.

$$2y - 2 = y + 6$$

Guidepost Methods for solving math equations.

For now, forget about what quantity y might represent and just focus on using the above relationship to determine what value of y will make the left side of the equation truly equal to the right side of the equation. To do that, it's important to keep the final goal in mind, which is to end up with $y =$ something. The reason we want to end up with $y =$ something is that it's then pretty easy to figure out what value of y will make the equality a true statement. Now that we have our goal, it's a matter of doing legal operations to this equation to get that result. Legal operations, at least as far as we've covered them, include adding the same quantity to both sides, subtracting the same quantity from both sides, multiplying both sides by the same quantity, or dividing both sides by the same quantity. All of those things will leave the equality intact, just as those things leave a double-pan balance in balance or leave two basketball teams in balance.

Okay, let's do something to both sides of our equation. I'm going to add the number 12 to both sides. We get

$2y - 2 = y + 6$

$2y - 2 + 12 = y + 6 + 12$

I can combine the numbers on each side and get

$2y + 10 = y + 18$

OK, that's really nice, but we are no closer to understanding what value of y will give us a true statement. All we've done is create a new equation. The reason I did this is to illustrate a basic concept in solving equations. You can do whatever you like to both sides and maintain the equality, but that doesn't necessarily mean you will get closer to a solution. How do you know what steps will get you closer to a solution? It takes a little thought, and often many blind alleys, before you know exactly what to do.

> **Guidepost** As long as you add the same thing to both sides of an equation or subtract the same thing from both sides of an equation, you maintain the equality.

In our current example, we have to keep the goal in mind. We want y all by itself on one side of the equation and other stuff on the other side of the equation. If we want just y on the left side, that means we should get rid of the – 2 on the left (talking about the original equation here, not the transformed one I got from adding 12 to both sides). What can we do to both sides of the equation that gets rid of the – 2 on the left? Because – 2 + 2 is equal to 0, and anything plus 0 is equal to the anything, it makes sense to simply add 2 to both sides of the equation.

$2y - 2 = y + 6$

$2y - 2 + 2 = y + 6 + 2$ adding 2 to both sides

$2y + 0 = y + 8$ replacing – 2 + 2 with 0 and adding 6 and 2 to get 8

$2y = y + 8$ using the fact that $2y + 0$ is equal to $2y$

We're closer to the goal, but not there yet. There's a $2y$ on the left side and a y on the right side. We need all of the y terms on the same side of the equation. Because you can add and subtract variables just as well as numbers, it makes sense to subtract y from both sides of the equation. When we do that, we'll get $y - y$ on the right, which is equal to 0, which is a good thing. So let's do that.

$2y = y + 8$

$2y - y = y - y + 8$ subtract y from both sides

$2y - y = 0 + 8$ because $y - y = 0$

Next we can combine the y terms on the left-hand side. $2y - y$ is equal to y.[*] Also, $0 + 8$ is equal to 8, so we have

$y = 8$

And we're done. If we put the number 8 in for y, we get a true statement, both with the simplified equation $y = 8$ and the original equation $2y - 2 = y + 6$.

Since that was so easy, let's try another one.

$3x + 15 = 0$

Once again, we want to get the variable (x in this case) all by itself on one side of the equation. To start with, I'm going to do a step that I highly recommend

---

[*] If you take one y away from two of them, you're left with one of them. Also, you can rewrite $2y$ - y as $2y + (-y)$ and figure it out from there.

you *not* do, which is to take the 15 to the opposite side of the equation and make it negative.

$3x + 15 = 0$ then becomes $3x = -15$. This new equation happens to be correct, but the shortcut of "taking something to the opposite side and making it negative" can lead to lots of confusion. Besides, it makes no sense. Do you remember when I told you to take a nut from one side of the double-pan balance to the other side and cause it to have the opposite effect it had on the first side? I did that to point out what a silly notion that was.[*] How can the nut have a negative effect on the balance? It would have to have a negative weight. Now, numbers are different from nuts, in that they can easily be negative. For that reason, the shortcut does work. However, I'm going to recommend that you stick with things that make sense, such as doing the same operation on each side of an equation. Before we do that, I should mention that, back in the Mesozoic Era when I was in elementary school, it was common to teach people to take a term to the opposite side of the equation and make it negative. You don't often see that in textbooks anymore, but some teachers still teach that technique to students. Bad teachers. Bad teachers.

OK, let's solve that second equation using techniques that make sense. To get the 15 on the right-hand side of the equation, we can subtract 15 from both sides. That gives us

$3x + 15 = 0$

$3x + 15 - 15 = 0 - 15$ subtracting 15 from both sides

$3x + 0 = -15$ because $15 - 15$ is equal to 0 and $0 - 15$ is equal to -15

$3x = -15$ because $3x + 0$ is equal to $3x$

OK, we're at the point we would have been had we just taken the 15 to the opposite side and made it negative. More steps, yes, but also steps that make sense. Of course, we're not done. We know what $3x$ needs to be in order for this equality to be a true statement, but we don't know what x has to be in order to have a legitimate equality. I know, you can probably figure out already that you have a true statement when x is equal to -5, but I'm trying to illustrate a process here. The answers won't be obvious with more complicated equations. So anyway, we have

$3x = -15$.

---

[*] Actually, if you're clever you might decide to push up with the nut on the opposite side with a force just equal to the nut's weight, but then you would be helping the process rather than having the nut do it all by itself.

I have actually had students do the following at this point: "I need to get the 3 on the other side of the equation, so I'm going to take it to the other side and make it negative." They end up with $x = -15 - 3$. That's definitely wrong, and it can show what happens in the extreme when you follow rules without understanding the rules. So how can we get rid of the 3 from the left side? Here we rely on the fact that a number times its reciprocal equals 1, or equivalently, a number divided by itself equals 1. I can multiply both sides of the equation by $\frac{1}{3}$, as in

$$\frac{1}{3} \cdot 3x = \frac{1}{3} \cdot (-15)$$

> **Guidepost** Multiplying both sides of an equation by the same thing or dividing both sides of an equation by the same thing maintains the equality.

$x = -5$ because $\frac{1}{3} \cdot 3$ equals 1 and $\frac{1}{3} \cdot (-15)$ equals -5.

The equivalent of multiplying by a number's reciprocal is dividing by the number itself. So, we can just divide both sides of our original equation by 3.

$3x = -15$

$\dfrac{3x}{3} = \dfrac{-15}{3}$ divide both sides by 3

$x = -5$ because $\dfrac{3}{3}$ equals 1 and $\dfrac{-15}{3}$ equals -5.

I'll address more complicated examples in the Applications section, but the basic process is always the same. You combine terms and simplify whenever it helps, and then you perform operations to both sides of the equation until you get to a final answer. As with much of what I cover in this book, understanding the meaning behind the rules puts you way ahead of the game, but if you want to *do* math proficiently, then you have to follow that understanding with lots and lots of practice on the procedures.

More things to do before you read more explanation

Back in Chapter 5 I introduced you to a math relationship that you could use to determine how long it would take for an object to fall under the influence of gravity from a given height. What I didn't show you was that I started with one relationship and did a few manipulations before coming up with the relationship I showed you. Time to remedy that just a bit. If you drop an object from rest at a height h above the ground, the height is related to the time of fall t by*

$$h = ½(10)t^2$$

If I want to solve this relationship for t, meaning I want an expression like $t =$ something, I'm going to have to first multiply both sides by 2, which gets rid of the ½ on the right side, and then divide both sides by 10. Here are those steps.

$h = ½(10)t^2$

$2h = 2 \cdot ½(10)t^2$ multiplying both sides by 2

$2h = (10)t^2$ because $2 \cdot ½$ is equal to 1

$\dfrac{2h}{10} = \dfrac{10t^2}{10}$ dividing both sides by 10

$\dfrac{2h}{10} = t^2$ because $\dfrac{10}{10}$ is equal to 1

Now it doesn't make any difference what's on the left side and what's on the right side as long as we maintain the equality, so I'm going to rearrange that equation to read

$$t^2 = \frac{2h}{10}$$

Lest you think I wasn't going to have you do anything in this "things to do" section, here's a challenge. See if you can figure out what you need to do to both sides of this equation to solve for t. I'm asking you to come up with $t =$ something, where the something involves numbers and variables (specifically the variable h) and maybe other math symbols. Take an honest stab at it before you read further, OK?

More explanation

Here's our equation

$$t^2 = \frac{2h}{10}$$

How can we get t when we have t^2? Well, if you take the square root of t^2 you get t, because the definition of a square root is the number you can multiply by itself to get what you're taking the square root of. Multiply t by itself and you

---

* I'm cringing just a bit as I write down this relationship. The last thing I want anyone to think is that knowing this relationship means you understand exactly what it is and where it comes from. Just as too many people memorize math, too many people memorize physics. So no, I don't expect that this relationship necessarily makes perfect sense to you. All I can say is that we're concentrating on the math and not the physical origin of this relationship. Also, remember that I'm using the number 10 to make the calculations easier. The true number is closer to 9.8.

get t^2, so that works. So, maybe if we took the square root of both sides of our equation, we could get what we're after. We have to be careful, though. Back when I introduced square roots, I talked about the fact that there is a positive square root and a negative square root, and that there is something called a radical that refers only to the positive square root. What should we do here—use the square root or use the radical? This brings up a big ol' dilemma. One of the esteemed reviewers of this book, a mathematician, correctly points out that mathematicians would use only the radical in doing something to both sides of an equation. If we combine that process with an operation known as *absolute value*, we can proceed with no problem and take into account all the positive and negative answers that might result. The dilemma arises because virtually all physics texts and other science texts use the process of taking the *square root* of both sides of an equation. Given this situation, I'm going to use the process of taking the square root of both sides. Mathematicians might wince at the lack of purity of this approach, but since this is a science book series, I'm going to stick with what scientists generally do.

Guidepost What happens when you take the square root of both sides of an equation.

So, let's start with our original equation and take the square root of both sides. Before doing that, I'll introduce a new notation. Taking the square root of a number results in both a positive and a negative answer. So, for example, $\sqrt{4}$ = +2 or -2. In order to avoid writing +2 or -2, we can write ±2, which is read "plus or minus 2."

$t^2 = \dfrac{2h}{10}$ the equation we're starting with

$\sqrt{t^2} = \sqrt{\dfrac{2h}{10}}$ taking the square root of both sides

$\pm t = \sqrt{\dfrac{2h}{10}}$ because the square root of t^2 has both a plus and minus answer

We're pretty much done. All we need to do is put in some value for h and we'll get an answer for the time. Let's suppose h (the height from which we drop the object) is 20 meters. Then we have

$\pm t = \sqrt{\dfrac{2h}{10}} = \sqrt{\dfrac{2 \cdot 20}{10}} = \sqrt{\dfrac{40}{10}} = \sqrt{4} = \pm 2$ because the square root of 2 has both a plus and minus answer.

We end up with

$\pm t = \pm 2$

What the heck does that mean? Well, we have to consider all the possibilities.

They are

$+t = +2$

$-t = +2$

$+t = -2$

$-t = -2$

Now this seems pretty complicated, but it's not as bad as it looks. Let's multiply both sides of the last equation by -1.

$-t = -2$

$(-1) \cdot (-t) = (-1) \cdot (-2)$ multiplying both sides by -1

$t = 2$ because $(-1) \cdot (-t)$ is equal to t and $(-1) \cdot (-2)$ is equal to 2 (a negative times a negative equals a positive—see Chapter 4).

So, the equation $-t = -2$ is the same equation as $t = 2$. Similarly, $-t = +2$ is the same equation as $t = -2$. To see that last one, multiply both sides of the equation $-t = +2$ by -1 and see what you get. At any rate, when we take the square root of both sides of $t^2 = 4$, we really only get two possible answers, which we can express as

$t = \pm 2.$

Well, that's certainly a relief. What we've learned is that there are two possible answers for the time it takes for an object to fall from a height of 20 meters. One answer is 2 seconds, and the other answer is negative 2 seconds! In other words, you simply go back in time two seconds, right?

It's time to let you in on a little secret. Scientists seldom have a problem taking the square root of both sides of an equation. If they get an answer that doesn't make sense, such as a negative time, then they usually just ignore that answer as physically unreasonable and move on. Of course, this answer of negative 2 seconds really is telling us something about the motion of things. The answer of +2 seconds tells us about the time it takes for a ball to fall 20 meters with only the force of gravity acting on it. See Figure 7.2.

When we put in a value of 20 meters for h and we use the number 10 in the denominator,

Figure 7.2

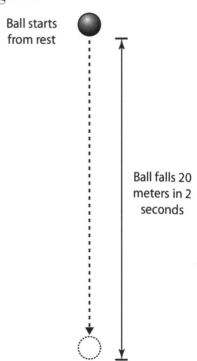

Ball starts from rest

Ball falls 20 meters in 2 seconds

we are specifying only the distance moved, the fact that gravity is the only force acting, and the fact that the object isn't moving at time $t = 0$.[*] However, those conditions also describe another possible motion, which is that of throwing the ball upward from the ground at just the right speed so it comes to rest exactly at height h. If gravity is again the only force acting during the motion, and $t = 0$ when the ball comes to rest, then the ball was thrown, and was h meters away from the highest height, at $t = -2$ seconds, or two seconds before the time $t = 0$. So, even though we're talking about simply dropping a ball and not throwing it upward from the ground, our math relationship is smarter than we are! The answer of $t = -2$ tells us there is a physical situation that meets our conditions that we're not considering. See Figure 7.3. As I said earlier, we are free to ignore that solution if it doesn't give us the answer we're looking for. Sometimes, though, we'd best not ignore that solution.

Here's an example of when it was smart of physicists not to ignore the negative solution when taking the square root of both sides of an equation. Physicists spend a lot of time studying subatomic particles—particles that are smaller than atoms. In case you didn't know it, there are hundreds of such particles, and they go by the name of protons, muons, neutrinos, and the like. When studying such things, it's revealing to study their energies. In fact there is a definite relationship between the energy of the particle, its mass, and its speed. I won't bother with the details of

Figure 7.3

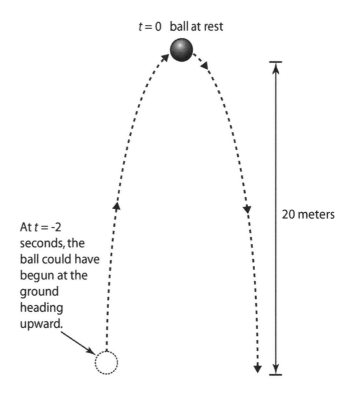

$t = 0$ ball at rest

20 meters

At $t = -2$ seconds, the ball could have begun at the ground heading upward.

---

[*] Again, you'll have to trust me that I've done this properly. What I'm using here is a special form of one of a set of equations called **kinematic equations**. Check out the first couple of chapters of any high school or college physics text and you'll find a thorough treatment of kinematic equations.

that relationship, but I will tell you that it looks like

E^2 = a bunch of other things squared

where E represents the energy of the particle.

> **Guidepost** An example of when taking the square root of both sides of an equation leads to a meaningful result.

In order to solve for the energy, E, you take the square root of both sides of the equation. As always happens when you take the square root of both sides of an equation, you get a positive answer and a negative answer. The negative answer in this case seems a bit silly. How can something have negative energy?* Well, just as with the falling ball, it turns out that the negative answer was telling physicists something when they came across it. You can interpret the negative energy as a particle with positive energy moving backward in time. Even stranger, it turns out that a particle moving backward in time is equivalent to that same particle with an opposite electrical charge moving forward in time. The particles we end up with this manipulation of negative energies and backward-moving time are called **antiparticles**. There are anti-protons, anti-electrons (called positrons), anti-muons, etc. These antiparticles are essential for a coherent theory of how the subatomic world behaves.

> I really should say something about scientific theories at this point. As I have said in other books in this series, all of science is made up. Scientific theories have not been handed down from on high, but rather have been invented by people.[†] As such, these theories don't always make common sense. As long as they do a good job of explaining observations and predicting new observations, they're good theories. It doesn't matter whether or not you believe these theories are actually true, as long as they work. Hey, if a model that includes antiparticles moving backward in time helps form a coherent theory, then it's, as Martha Stewart would say, a good thing.

Even more things to do before you read even more explanation

See if you can write an equation to represent the following scenario: Suppose we define as rich anyone who has over a million dollars. If we let d be a variable

---

* Specifically ignoring teenagers on a summer day, here.

---

† As a qualifier, I should state that this is my own philosophical view of things. There are plenty of scientists out there who believe that scientific theories are out there waiting for people to discover them, rather than being things that people invent.

that represents how much money someone has,* use *d* in an equation that describes how much money rich people have. Yeah, I know that's not much to go on, but try it anyway.

Let's go back to our basketball teams from earlier in the chapter. Now though, let's have one team, Team A, that is clearly inferior to another team, Team B. In terms of quality, we could say that Team A clearly is *less than* Team B. No, that's not great grammar, but it serves our purpose. See Figure 7.4.

Figure 7.4

is less than

Team A   Team B

Here's what I want you to do. Imagine that you have a magic wand that makes teams the opposite of what they are. If you have a great team, waving the wand will cause it to be an awful team. If you have an awful team, waving the wand will cause it to be a great team. It's sort of like the Los Angeles Clippers (pick any Clipper team you like!) trading places with the Chicago Bulls when they had Michael Jordan. How would Figure 7.4 change in response to your magic wand?

---

* Sometimes people get hung up on the particular letters used for variables, thinking that *x* always has to represent one kind of variable, *y* another kind of variable, and so on. While scientists and mathematicians sometimes establish *conventions* for what variables should be used when, there really are no hard and fast rules. Whenever you see a variable, just make sure you know what quantity it represents. Also be aware that using Greek symbols such as θ, γ, ρ, ω, and ψ for variables is common when dealing with geometry, higher math, and physics.

Even more explanation

How did you do with the challenge to write an equation describing the amount of money rich people have? Maybe not very well, given that I misled you. It's impossible to write an *equation* for that relationship, because there isn't one amount of money you can have to be considered rich. All amounts over one million dollars work. Therefore, we need something besides an equals sign. In words (which is how you should first write equations that represent the real world), the relationship is

amount of money rich people have *is greater than* one million dollars

Lucky for us, there's a special math symbol for *is greater than*. It's (>). With this symbol, our word equation becomes

amount of money rich people have > one million dollars

Now, since I told you to let *d* represent the amount of money rich people have, this becomes

d > 1,000,000

Whenever you have a relationship that involves the symbols > or < (the latter symbol means *less than*), that's known as an **inequality**.

Guidepost   The definition of an inequality.

Let's suppose the inequality you have isn't as simple as $d > 1,000,000$. What if it looks like the following:

$4x + 4 < 12x + 2x$

How do you solve inequalities like this? Basically, you solve them the same way you solve equations, with one major exception. I'll point out that exception when we get to it. In the meantime, let's go ahead and solve this inequality. First, notice that there are two *x* terms on the right side that we can combine.

$4x + 4 < 12x + 2x$ original inequality

$4x + 4 < 14x$ combine the 12x and 2x to get 14x

Next we move toward the goal of getting the *x* all by itself on one side, just as we would with an equation. In order to get rid of the 4 from the left side, I'm going to subtract 4 from both sides. This is okay to do, because if you have two teams, one worse than the other one, subtracting equal quality players from both teams will maintain the relationship. The team that is worse to start with will still be worse.

$4x + 4 - 4 < 14x - 4$

$4x < 14x - 4$ because 4 – 4 is equal to zero, and $4x + 0$ equals $4x$

For the next step, there are two possible things to do. We could subtract $4x$ from both sides. That would get rid of the $4x$ from the left and get all the x terms on the right. The other thing we can do is subtract $14x$ from both sides, which will get rid of the $14x$ from the right side and get all the x terms on the left. That's what I'm going to do, because it leads to the exception I referred to earlier.

Guidepost   Solving inequalities.

$4x - 14x < 14x - 14x - 4$ subtract $14x$ from both sides

$4x - 14x < 0 - 4$ because $14x - 14x$ is equal to 0

$-10x < -4$ because $4x - 14x$ is equal to $-10x$ and $0 - 4$ is equal to -4

$\dfrac{-10x}{10} < \dfrac{-4}{10}$ dividing both sides by 10 to get x by itself on the left

$-x < \dfrac{-2}{5}$ because $\dfrac{10}{10}$ is equal to 1, and $\dfrac{-4}{10}$ is the same as $\dfrac{-2}{5}$

OK, now we know what $-x$ is less than, but what we want to solve for is x, not $-x$. To get $-x$, we need to multiply both sides by -1. Fine, but we're at the exception. Think back to the two teams, A and B. Team A is worse than Team B. Even though the grammar isn't quite correct, we can say that

Team A *is less than* Team B

Remember the magic wand? When you wave it, it makes teams the opposite of what they were. So, if we wave the wand, Team A becomes a good team, and Team B becomes a bad team. After waving our wand, the original statement is no longer true. In fact, now that we have waved the wand, we have

Team A *is greater than* Team B

Now let's apply that reasoning to our inequality, which is

$-x < \dfrac{-2}{5}$

We decided that to get x by itself, we have to multiply each side by -1. Multiplying by -1 is the same as simply taking the negative of each side, because $1 \cdot$ (anything) equals the anything, and we still have that negative sign hanging around. Well, when you take the negative of something in math, that's the same as taking the *opposite* of it (see Chapter 4). We saw with the teams that taking the opposite of both sides of an inequality means the inequality changes. That gives us the following rule:

When you multiply or divide an inequality by a negative number, the direction of the inequality changes.

Guidepost The reasoning behind the rule that the direction of an inequality changes whenever you multiply or divide both sides by a negative number.

Applying this rule to our equation, we get

$$-x < \frac{-2}{5}$$

$(-1) \cdot (-x) > (-1) \cdot (\frac{-2}{5})$ change the direction of the < because we multiplied by a negative.

$$x > \frac{2}{5}$$

This is one of those rules that people often follow only because it's the rule, but if you remember the analogy with unequal teams, you can reason your way through the rule. Of course, you can always use a simple example. Start with a true statement such as 3 < 6. Well, 3 *is* less than 6, so this is true. Now multiply both sides by -3. You get -9 on the left and -18 on the right. If we keep the inequality as is, we get the *incorrect* statement that -9 is less than -18. -9 is *to the right* of -18 on the number line, so -9 is in fact *greater than* -18. See Figure 7.5.

Figure 7.5

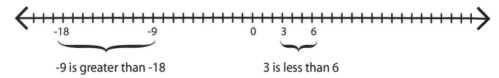

-9 is greater than -18   3 is less than 6

Here's the math.

3 < 6

$(-3) \cdot (3) > (-3) \cdot (6)$ The inequality changes direction as soon as you multiply by a negative number.

-9 > -18   A true statement.

As your homework assignment, try dividing both sides of 3 < 6 by -3. Convince yourself that you only get a true statement if you change the < to > when you do the division.

Chapter Summary

- When two expressions are equal, doing the same thing to both expressions generally maintains the equality.

- The above statement applies to math equations. When you perform the same math operation to both sides of an equation, you maintain the equality.

- To solve an equation, you do the same thing to both sides of the equation until you get the desired variable all by itself on one side of the equation.

- There usually are many paths that lead to a correct solution of an equation.

- Taking the square root of both sides of an equation often leads to two possible solutions, each of which might or might not be meaningful.

- You solve inequalities in the same way that you solve equations, with one exception: When you multiply or divide both sides of an inequality by a negative number, the direction of the inequality changes.

Applications

1. In Chapter 6, we arrived at an equation that describes the process of adding antifreeze of one concentration to antifreeze of a different concentration to get a final solution. That equation is below.

$$0.25 \cdot 10 + 0.1x = 0.15 \cdot (10 + x)$$

If you look back at this problem in Chapter 6, you'll find that x represents the number of liters of 10% solution. So, we should solve for x. The first thing to do is a bit of a neat trick that will get rid of those nasty decimals. The basis of the trick is that you can multiply something like 0.25 by the number 100 and change it to a number without decimals, as in $100 \cdot 0.25 = 25$. If you need a quick review of why multiplying by 100 moves the decimal point two places, head back to Chapter 2. Anyway, I'm going to multiply both sides of the above equation by 100.

$$0.25 \cdot 10 + 0.1x = 0.15 \cdot (10 + x)$$

$$100 \cdot [0.25 \cdot 10 + 0.1x] = 100 \cdot 0.15 \cdot (10 + x)$$

Notice that I used brackets [ ] to indicate that we have to multiply *everything* on the left side of the equation by 100, not just one or two select terms. On the left side, I'm going to use the distributive property first.* Then we have

$$100 \cdot 0.25 \cdot 10 + 100 \cdot 0.1x = 100 \cdot 0.15 \cdot (10 + x)$$

---

* A general statement of the distributive property is $a \cdot (b + c) = a \cdot b + a \cdot c$.

2. Next I'm going to multiply 100 times 0.25 in the first term on the left, 100 times 0.1 in the second term on the left, and 100 times 0.15 in the term on the right. That gives

$$25 \cdot 10 + 10x = 15 \cdot (10 + x)$$

Next I'll do a multiplication on the left and again use the distributive property on the right.

$$25 \cdot 10 + 10x = 15 \cdot (10 + x)$$

$250 + 10x = 15 \cdot 10 + 15x$	multiplied on left and used distributive property on right
$250 + 10x = 150 + 15x$	multiplied on the right

Now that we've done all those steps, we have an equation that looks a whole lot easier to solve. Given that you're really good at this by now, I'll just do the necessary steps and explain out to the side as I continue.

$250 + 10x = 150 + 15x$	
$250 - 150 + 10x = 150 - 150 + 15x$	subtract 150 from each side
$100 + 10x = 15x$	perform subtractions
$100 + 10x - 10x = 15x - 10x$	subtract 10x from both sides
$100 = 5x$	perform subtractions
$\dfrac{100}{5} = \dfrac{5x}{5}$	divide both sides by 5 to get x by itself on the right side
$20 = x$	perform divisions, noting that $\dfrac{5}{5}$ is equal to 1

So our answer is that x is equal to 20 liters. That means you have to add 20 liters of the 10% solution to the 10 liters of 25% solution to get a solution that is 15% antifreeze. By the way, since there are $x + 10$ liters of the final solution, you end up with 30 liters of 15% solution. In all word problems, you should check to see whether the answer makes sense. Since the final solution of 15% is closer in concentration to the 10% solution than the 25% solution, it makes sense that you should have more liters of the 10% solution than of the 25% solution.

3. We set up a few equations in the previous chapter that represented the conditions when two trains set out from separate cities at different speeds, traveling toward each other. The *distance = rate · time* relationship gave us

$d_1 = r_1t_1$ and $d_2 = r_2t_2$ for trains 1 and 2. The other information in the problem gave us

$$40 \cdot t_1 + 60 \cdot t_2 = 50$$

and

$$t_1 = t_2 .$$

Since $t_1 = t_2$, we can rewrite

$$40 \cdot t_1 + 60 \cdot t_2 = 50$$

as

$40t + 60t = 50$ where we're just using t without subscripts because the times are the same

Next we can combine the two terms on the left and get

$100t = 50$ because $40t + 60t = 100t$

Next just divide both sides by 100 to get the t by itself.

$$\frac{100t}{100} = \frac{50}{100}$$

$t = \frac{1}{2}$ or 0.5 because the 100s cancel on the left

Before continuing, what does that 0.5 mean? 0.5 seconds? 0.5 days? Aside from the fact that both those answers are downright silly, we note that the speeds were given in miles per *hour,* so the time until the trains meet is 0.5 hours. The next thing to do is calculate d_1 and d_2.

$$d_1 = r_1t_1 = (40)(0.5) = 20 \text{ miles}$$

$$d_2 = r_2t_2 = (60)(0.5) = 30 \text{ miles}$$

As always, we should check to see that the answers make sense. They do, because the total distance between the cities is 50 miles.

4. Often in math you will see an equation such as $\frac{3}{8} = \frac{4}{x}$. You probably learned a method for simplifying this known as **cross multiplying**. When you cross multiply in the above equation, you get $3x = 8 \cdot 4$. As a more general expression of this shortcut, we can say that $\frac{a}{b} = \frac{c}{d}$ becomes $ad = bc$ after cross multiplying. But why does this shortcut work? It's really just an application of what we've learned in this chapter. What I'm going to do is start with $\frac{a}{b} = \frac{c}{d}$ and do things to both sides of the equation.

$$\frac{a}{b} = \frac{c}{d}$$

$$\frac{a}{b} \cdot d = \frac{c}{d} \cdot d \qquad \text{multiply both sides by } d$$

$$\frac{a}{b} \cdot d = c \qquad \text{because the } d\text{'s on the right cancel}$$

$$b \cdot \frac{a}{b} \cdot d = b \cdot c \qquad \text{multiply both sides by } b$$

$$a \cdot d = b \cdot c \qquad \text{because the } b\text{'s on the left cancel}$$

$ad = bc \qquad$ rewrite without the dots, because two letters next to each other implies multiplication.

And that's the result: Another shortcut that can be explained by applying basic concepts.

Parental Warning–
Graphic Math

Being the clever person you are, you no doubt guessed from the title that this chapter is about graphs. Of course, it won't be the standard coverage of graphs that you find in textbooks. I'm not going to spend a whole lot of time on plotting points on x and y axes, because that's something you can learn in lots of places. What I will cover are topics that seem to confuse people, largely because they try to memorize procedures, rather than understand what's going on. So, while I'll address many issues related to graphs, this chapter won't look like the typical chapter on graphing from a math textbook.

"I just realized we've been drawing these graphs backward!"

Things to do before you read the explanation

Imagine you own your own business and make lots of money. In keeping track of that money, there's an important quantity you need to calculate periodically. That quantity is known as the *cost of goods sold*. Since you make lots of money, you want to make sure that you take more money in than you spend on what you sell. Well, for any period of time, say a month, the cost of goods is determined by a few things. Obviously one of those is the money you spend on purchases. Another is the difference between the value of your inventory at the beginning of the period and the value of your inventory at the end of the period. Here's your task. See if you can write an equation that shows how the cost of goods sold depends on those quantities. In other words, you're after an equation that looks like

Cost of goods sold = some math expression involving cost of purchases and the value of inventory at the beginning and end of the period in question

As a hint, it's not a complicated equation.

Second task. What does the term *function* mean to you? Think of any examples from everyday life where you might have used the word *function*.

The explanation

Let's address the second task first. What does the word *function* mean? Chances are you thought of objects that "have a function," as in "the function of this thingamabob is to generate pure water from that filth that comes from your faucet." My daughter just said, when asked what the word means, "How something operates; its purpose." My wife said, "A tool, a method, or an instruction." Those two people represent a large portion of people who are reading this book, I think. The reason I think that is because both of them are quite intelligent, and both of them dislike math and science.

Guidepost The definition of a function.

The word **function** in math has a specialized meaning. To address that special meaning, I'll use the example of an equation for the cost of goods sold. I told you that the cost of goods sold is determined by the purchases you make in any period and the difference between the value of your inventory at the beginning of the period and the value at the end of the period. Another way of stating that is to say that the cost of goods sold *is a function of* those other things. Let's write a word equation for the relationship.

Cost of goods sold = (purchases made) + (difference between
inventory value at the beginning and end of the period)

We can make that more of a mathematical relationship by writing the difference as a subtraction, as in

Cost of goods sold = (purchases made) + (inventory value
at beginning – inventory value at end)

To make it even more like a regular old math equation, I'll use variables to represent the quantities. C will represent the cost of goods sold, P will represent the purchases, b will represent the inventory value at the beginning of the period, and e will represent the value of the inventory at the end of the period. Our equation then looks like the following:

$$C = P + (b - e)$$

Before going on, let's see if this makes sense. If you make any purchases, then obviously that adds to the cost of goods sold, so having P as a positive contribution makes sense. How about $b - e$? Well, if this number is positive, then the value of the inventory is smaller at the end of the period than at the beginning (e is smaller than b). That means you used some of your inventory for sales during the period, and that represents a cost. If $b - e$ is equal to zero, you didn't use any inventory, so that's not a cost during the time period. It makes sense that you would then add 0 to the cost of goods sold. If $b - e$ is negative, then the value of the inventory increased during the period. If $b - e$ is negative, then that subtracts from the overall cost of goods sold. You might have paid money to increase your inventory, and those purchases will show up in the variable P. Because you didn't actually sell those goods, though, it makes sense to subtract that value from the increase represented in P.

OK, let's just put in some numbers. Let's say that in a one-month period, you had purchases of $500,000 (told you that you made a lot of money in this business!). The value of your inventory at the beginning of the period was $2,000,000 and the value of your inventory at the end of the period was $1,700,000. Then you can calculate the cost of goods sold as

$C = P + (b - e)$

$C = 500,000 + (2,000,000 - 1,700,000)$

$C = \$800,000$

OK, so what? I did that simple calculation to demonstrate something, which is that for any set of values for P, b, and e, there is one unique answer for C. That's the main definition of a mathematical function. For each set of values that you plug in for your variables, you get one and only one answer. That might not seem all that important to you, but functions are nice things to have in science and in lots of other applications. In many situations, we use mathematical relationships to predict results. If a given set of conditions, represented by the values of a set of variables, doesn't give you a unique answer, then the predictive value of those variables is not very good.

As another example of a function, consider the relationship between the distance something falls from a resting state and the time it takes for it to fall that distance. The relationship is

$$h = \tfrac{1}{2}(10)t^2$$

Guidepost Another example of a function.

Previously, we used h to represent the total distance an object travels, from the point of release to the ground. However, this relationship works for any distance fallen. If you drop an object from 500 meters, you can find out how far it has fallen after 1 second, after 3 seconds, or after 5 seconds. No matter what number you put in for t, you get a unique value for h. That means that h is a function of the variable t, or that the distance fallen is a function of the time of fall.

Since this is a chapter about graphs, why not graph this function? For basics on graphing, take a look at any algebra textbook.* As a quick reminder, the relationship between two variables, such as our h and t, can be graphed using vertical and horizontal axes as in Figure 8.1.

To graph the relationship $h = \tfrac{1}{2}(10)t^2$, you simply choose a few values for t and calculate corresponding values for

Figure 8.1

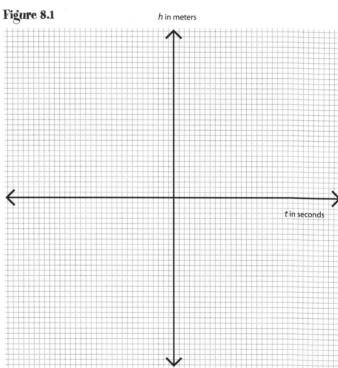

h in meters

t in seconds

---

* You absolutely must know how to plot data points on a grid in order to understand what follows. That means you can place a dot on a graph based on the ordered pair that describes the point, as in (3, 8) describing a point that is three places to the right from zero on the horizontal axis and eight places up from zero on the vertical axis.

h. When *t* is equal to zero, *h* is also equal to 0. Just in case you forgot how to calculate such things, that calculation is below.

$h = \frac{1}{2}(10)t^2$

$h = \frac{1}{2}(10)(0)^2$ substituting 0 for *t*

$h = \frac{1}{2}(10)(0)$ because 0^2 is equal to 0

$h = 0$ because 0 times anything is equal to 0

Of course, that answer makes sense. At time *t* = 0, the object hasn't started falling yet, so of course *h* will equal 0.

I'll let you go ahead and figure out that when *t* equals 1 second, *h* equals 5 meters; when *t* equals 2 seconds, *h* equals 20 meters; and when *t* equals 3 seconds, *h* equals 45 meters. Now we'll place those data points on our graph. Basically, you go to the right the number of spaces corresponding to the value of *t*, and then go straight up the number of spaces corresponding to the value of *h*. See Figure 8.2.

Figure 8.2

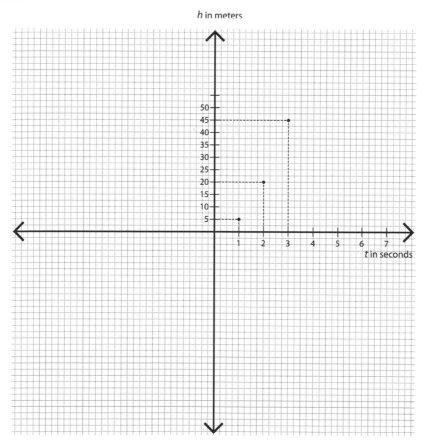

The next thing to do is draw a line that connects the points.* In this case, the line is a curved line, as shown in Figure 8.3. Note that this line goes through the point $h = 0$, $t = 0$, which fits our relationship.

Figure 8.3

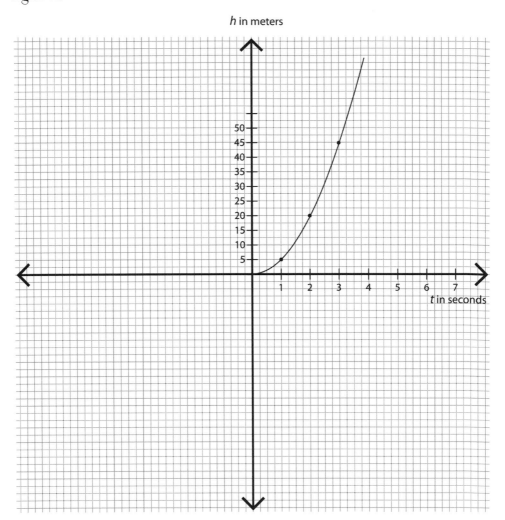

---

* In drawing such a line, we are stating that we are confident that all the points that are on the line satisfy our relationship. That's an easy claim to make here, because we can calculate as many values of h and t as we want and show they describe points on the line we draw. Sometimes, though, we don't have an exact relationship and are making the best guess we can as to the line that correctly describes a set of data points.

What I want you to notice about this graph is that each value of *t* is associated with only one value of *h,* meaning that this is a function. See Figure 8.4.

Figure 8.4

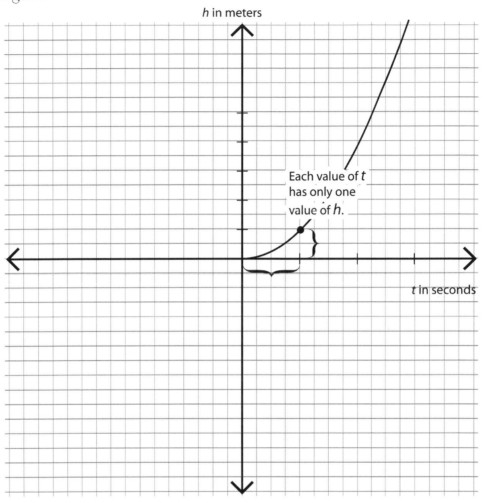

h in meters

Each value of *t* has only one value of *h.*

t in seconds

Guidepost   Using graphs to determine whether or not a math relationship is a function.

Just to be complete, I should address negative values of the time, *t.* In Chapter 7 I talked about what negative values of *t* mean. They are times before time zero, and apply to what might have happened if the object were thrown upward prior to being momentarily at rest. Since negative times do describe a possible physical situation, they should also be a part of the function. In fact, they are. Figure 8.5 shows the graph of $h = \frac{1}{2}(10)t^2$ when negative values of t are included. As shown in that figure, we still have a function, because for each value of t, there is one and only one value of h.

Figure 8.5

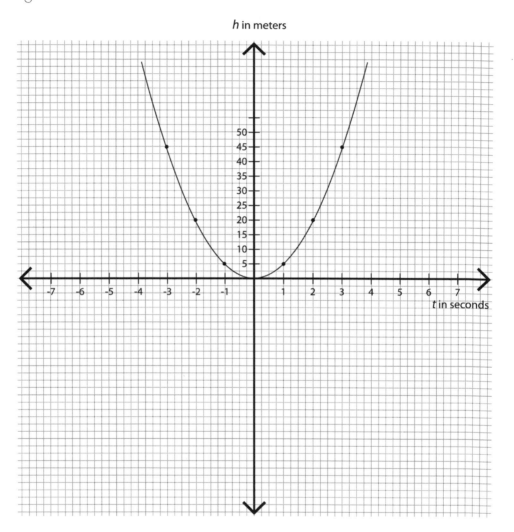

h in meters

t in seconds

When you have a graph of a relationship, it's easy to decide whether or not what you have is a function. Just draw any old vertical line you want (here that means you pick a value of the time, t, and draw a vertical line through that point). If that vertical line crosses the graph at more than one point, you don't have a function. Figure 8.6 shows this as applied to our graph of *h* and *t*.[*]

Figure 8.6

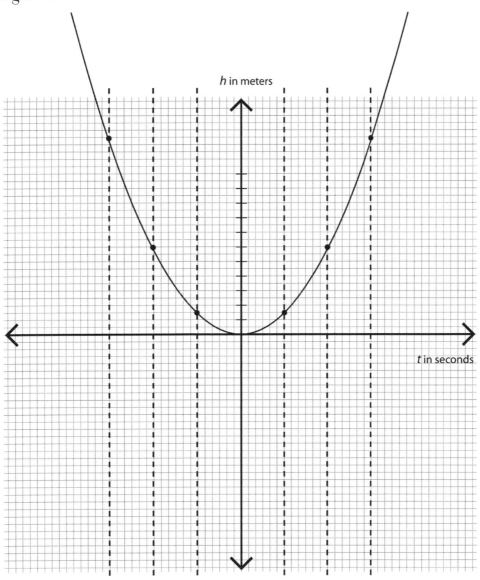

Each vertical line crosses the graph in only one place.

---

[*] Think about what it would mean for a vertical line to cross our graph in more than one place. That would mean that the object would be at two different heights at the same time.

Now let's look at something that doesn't qualify as a function, namely the relationship you get when you solve the distance and time relationship for t. We did that in Chapter 7, and the result is $t = \sqrt{\frac{2h}{10}}$. Let's interpret that as being the square root (both plus and minus values) rather than the radical (only the positive square root).[*] If we graph this relationship, it looks like Figure 8.7.

Figure 8.7

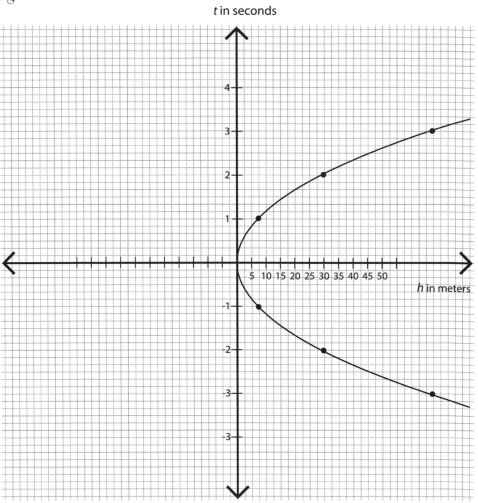

Guidepost An example of a math relationship that's not a function.

---

[*] Here again I am sticking with what scientists usually do, which is to deal with the square root rather than the radical. As we saw in an earlier chapter, one should always at least consider the possibility that the negative square root solution is telling you something that is physically important.

Notice that I've switched what the vertical and horizontal axes represent. That's because it's customary to plot the **independent variable** on the horizontal axis and the **dependent variable** on the vertical axis. I guess I better follow that statement with a definition of what independent and dependent variables are. The independent variable is the one you assign various values. You then calculate the value of the dependent variable based on the value of the independent variable. So, the value of the dependent variable *depends* on the value of the independent variable. In our current example, we can choose either *h* or *t* to be the dependent variable, depending on how we look at the situation. We can say that the distance something has fallen depends on the time since release, or we can say that the time since release can be determined by how far the object has fallen.

Of course, many times the independent and dependent variables are not interchangeable. An example of variables that aren't interchangeable is the relationship between how much you study for a test and the grade you get on the test. The grade is a function of the amount of study, so the grade is the dependent variable. You would never say that how much you study depends on the grade you get on the test, so how much you study can't be the dependent variable. The grade you get on the test cannot retroactively affect how much you study.[*]

Guidepost   Definition of independent and dependent variables.

Anyway, back to Figure 8.7. Notice that each value of *h* has two corresponding values of *t*. Any vertical line that passes through one point on the graph also passes through a second point on the graph. See Figure 8.8, next page.

---

[*] Of course you can play games with the wording here, and state that how much you *must* have studied for the test is a function of the grade you got on the test. In general, though, the independent variable is something you can deliberately vary, with a resultant variation in the dependent variable.

Figure 8.8

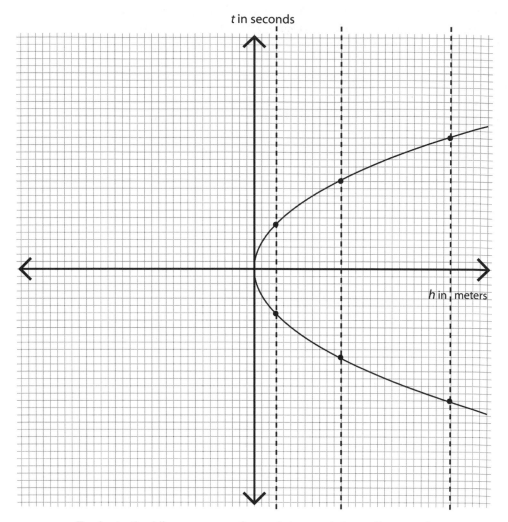

Each vertical line crosses through two points on the graph.

What this means is that $t = \sqrt{\frac{2h}{10}}$ is not a function in the mathematical sense. We can make it into a function, though, if we make that symbol on the right represent a radical rather than a square root. The graph of $t = \sqrt{\frac{2h}{10}}$ looks like Figure 8.9 when we use the radical rather than the square root.

Figure 8.9

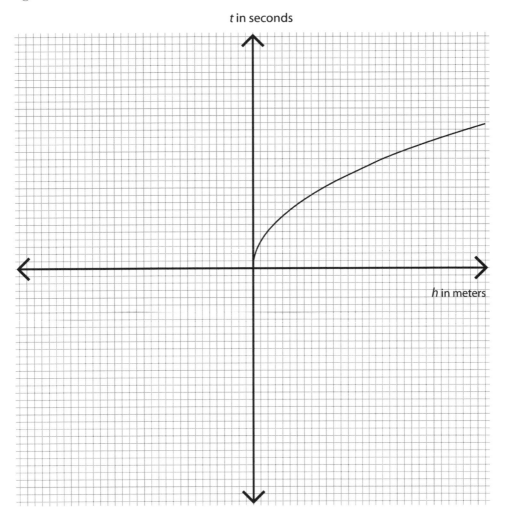

t in seconds

h in meters

That's a good thing to do if we want to restrict ourselves to the actual physical situation we're studying. We dropped the object from rest. We didn't throw it upward from the ground. So, while allowing negative values of the square root gives us a result we can interpret, using the radical and allowing only positive square roots accurately describes our situation.

More things to do before you read more explanation

Figure 8.10 shows a plot of fictitious data relating people's yearly income to the number of years of education they have. Even though I made up those data points, go ahead and pretend they're from an actual survey.

Figure 8.10

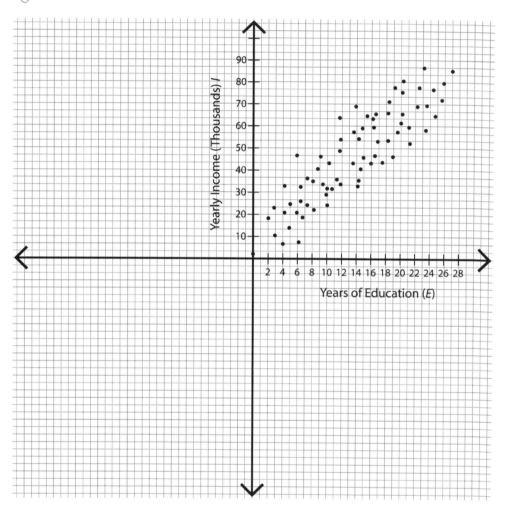

When scientists, economists, and other people who study data see something like Figure 8.10, they look for patterns in the data. Even though the data in our graph don't lie exactly along a straight line, they suggest a **linear relationship**

between the two variables. So, we're going to draw a line that seems to show the general trend of the data,* as in Figure 8.11.

Figure 8.11

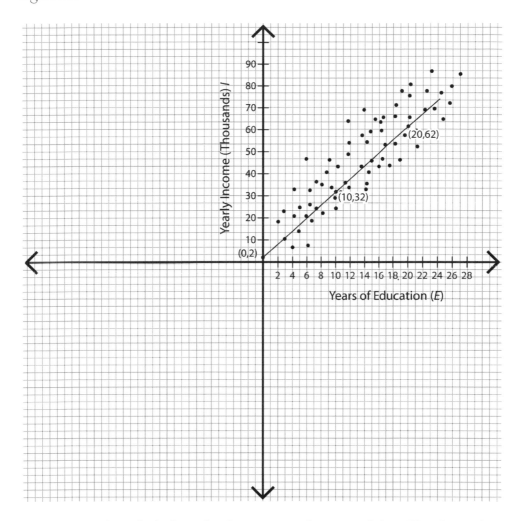

Figure 8.11 is typical of graphs that one gets from actual data. The data points suggest a linear relationship so much that we draw a line and use that line as a model for the data. In fact, we can write an equation that describes the line. It's

$$I = 3000E + 2000$$

where *I* stands for yearly income and *E* stands for years of education. Yeah, I know, as a teacher you can already see that this equation doesn't accurately describe all professions!

---

* For the record, the word *data* is plural, referring to more than one data point.

Here's your challenge. If in fact there is an actual linear relationship between education and yearly income, then why don't all these data points lie exactly on the line we draw? Think about this for a while, and try to come up with a deeper answer than "it's due to human error" or "people lied in the survey."

More explanation

Before addressing why all those points don't lie directly on the line drawn, notice that the line representing the data is a function. For each value of years of education, there is only one value for yearly income. That's good for the predictive value of the graph, but it also points out the difference between actual data and a model we create to represent the data. Obviously in reality there are many possible yearly incomes for a given number of years of education. The data on our fictitious graph even show that. There are many places where the data points lie along a vertical line. Anyway, this brings us to one answer as to why the data points don't all lie on the line. It's because we are modeling reality with a mathematical relationship, and that is never an exact process, even when talking about highly controlled scientific experiments. So, our line that represents the data is a function, but the actual data themselves cannot be called a function.

Okay, why else do the data points not lie on the line? Does it simply mean that our model (the line and the equation that describes it) is bad? Nah, just incomplete. Years of education isn't the only thing that might affect yearly income. Your chosen field of work, your age, where you live, and all other kinds of things affect your yearly income. A model that predicts income based solely on education doesn't include all these other variables, so there's no reason to expect that the data will follow this model exactly.

> **Guidepost**   How to interpret graphs that are drawn through actual data.

Even more things to do before you read even more explanation

A simple homework assignment for you. Find an algebra textbook and look up the following items: the slope of a line, the point-slope equation of a line, and the y-intercept equation of a line. No need to read through the entire chapter where these things are introduced unless you have a particularly strong need for textbook information right now. While you're looking at that textbook, make sure you understand what an **ordered pair** is, and how it is used to identify a point on the grid defined by a vertical and a horizontal axis.

Even more explanation

I'm going to start this section with a definition of the slope of a line, and then show how that slope definition leads to the different kinds of equations for lines. This is done in most math textbooks, but it's a pet peeve of mine that the process usually is not explained well. So, I'm going to take a shot at making the process more understandable.

Before starting, I should explain one convention about graphing. Whenever you don't have specific quantities in mind, such as with our cost of goods example, it's customary to use the variable *y* to represent the quantity on the vertical axis

Figure 8.12

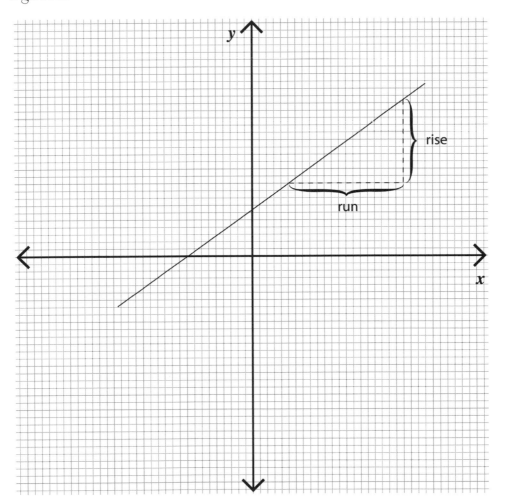

and the variable x to represent the quantity on the horizontal axis. That said, here's the definition of the slope of a line.[*]

Guidepost   Definition of the slope of a line.

$$\text{Slope} = \frac{\text{rise}}{\text{run}}$$

Figure 8.12 illustrates this definition.

To see that this definition makes sense, think about the word *slope* as it applies to your everyday life. A roof has a slope to it, a ski slope can be gradual or steep, and you can slope a driveway or parking lot so the rain runs off of it. If you have a steep slope, then for every bit you move horizontally, you move a lot vertically. If you have a small slope, then for every bit you move horizontally, you don't move much vertically. Take a look at Figure 8.13.

Figure 8.13

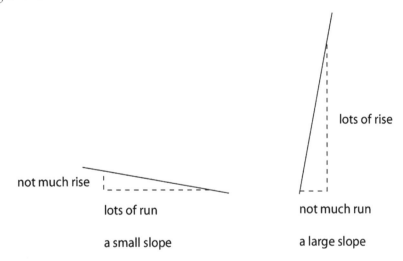

not much rise

lots of run

a small slope

lots of rise

not much run

a large slope

---

[*] In defining slope as rise divided by run, we have a potential source of confusion. If a line slopes upward to the right, then rise and run are no problem. If the line slopes downward to the right, then it doesn't rise, but in fact "drops." There's a simple way to deal with this. If the line slopes downward as it goes to the right, we simply say that the rise is a negative number. A general rule to follow is that lines that slope upward as they go to the right have a positive slope and lines that slope downward as they go to the right have a negative slope.

A more detailed definition of slope involves specific points on the line. I'm going to choose the points (2, 4) and (3, 8), which you will recognize as ordered pairs since I asked you to look that up in the previous section. Figure 8.14 shows those points on our line, and also the rise and the run.

Figure 8.14

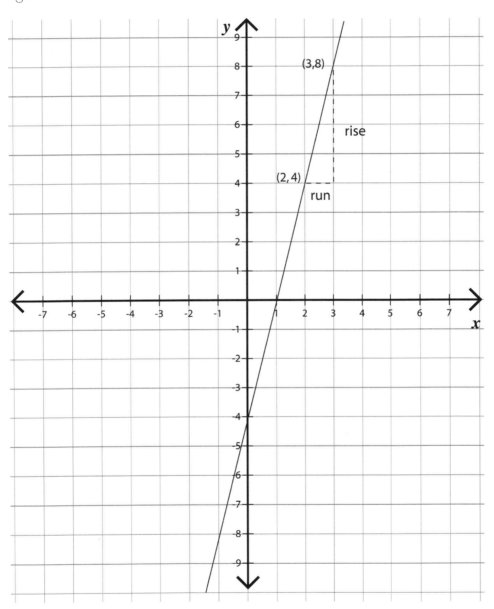

Now our slope is just[*]

$$\text{Slope} = \frac{\text{rise}}{\text{run}} = \frac{\text{difference in y values}}{\text{difference in x values}} = \frac{8-4}{3-2} = \frac{4}{1} = 4$$

If you want, you can pick any other two points on the line and find out that the slope is the same no matter what two points you choose. The slope is constant. That suggests that we can produce a more general expression for the slope of the line. What we're going to do is choose two arbitrary points on the line and call them (x_1, y_1) and (x_2, y_2). The subscripts in this case mean that we are referring to specific points, but that those points are arbitrary. If we specify an ordered pair (x, y), without subscripts, then the x and y represent all possible points on the line, not just specific ones. Hopefully, Figures 8.15 and 8.16, on the next two pages, clear this up.

Before supplying a general expression for slope, you need to know that the letter m is generally used to represent slope. So, our expression for the slope of a line is now

$$\text{Slope} = \frac{\text{rise}}{\text{run}} = \frac{y_2 - y_1}{x_2 - x_1} \quad \text{or} \quad m = \frac{y_2 - y_1}{x_2 - x_1}$$

That last relationship on the right is what you will find in any math text that discusses slope. What isn't always clear in those texts, though, is that this definition is the starting point for all of the different equations that describe lines. For starters, let's multiply both sides of the slope relationship by the quantity $x_2 - x_1$.

$$(x_2 - x_1) \cdot m = (x_2 - x_1)\left(\frac{y_2 - y_1}{x_2 - x_1}\right)$$

On the right, the $x_2 - x_1$ terms cancel out, so we're left with

$$(x_2 - x_1) \cdot m = \cancel{(x_2 - x_1)}\left(\frac{y_2 - y_1}{\cancel{x_2 - x_1}}\right)$$

$$(x_2 - x_1) \cdot m = y_2 - y_1$$

Guidepost Using the definition of slope to derive the point-slope equation for a line.

---

[*] You might remember our previous potential for confusion in using rise divided by run for slope, and how that relates to positive and negative slopes. If you simply use the difference in y values divided by the difference in x values, the sign of the slope (plus or minus) will come out properly.

Figure 8.15

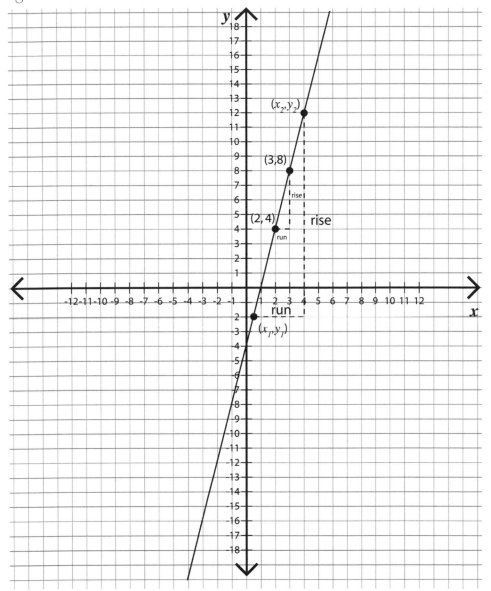

Now I'm going to do a couple of things. One is to switch the order of a couple of terms (the $x_2 - x_1$ and the m) and the other is to switch the left and right sides of the equation.

$$y_2 - y_1 = m(x_2 - x_1)$$

In this form, the statement is true for any two particular points, (x_1, y_1) and (x_2, y_2), on our line. To make this even more general, I'm going to replace the point

(x_2, y_2) with (x, y). That might seem like a trivial change, but since the variables x and y represent all points on the line rather than a specific point, we will end up with a relationship that is true for all of the points on the line. Of course, if the equation is true for any arbitrary specific points on the line, then it must also be true for all points on the line. See Figure 8.16.

Figure 8.16

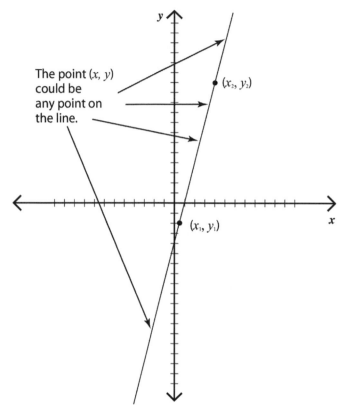

The point (x, y) could be any point on the line.

(x_2, y_2)

(x_1, y_1)

Now our equation reads

$$y - y_1 = m(x - x_1)$$

This is known as the point-slope form of the equation of a line. What I want you to realize is that this equation didn't come out of mid-air. It follows directly from the definition of the slope of a line. If you check back with your algebra textbook, you'll find that all you need to do to obtain an equation of a particular line is to substitute the value of the slope for m and substitute the coordinates of a particular point for x_1 and y_1. In our example, we already calculated the slope to be 4. We can use either of our points, (2, 4) or (3, 8), to get values for x_1 and y_1. I'll use (2, 4).

$$y - y_1 = m(x - x_1)$$
$$y - 4 = 4(x - 2)$$

And that's the point-slope form of the equation of our line.

Now, starting from the point-slope form of the equation of a line, we can move to the slope-intercept form. Before we move, though, I need to define something called the *y*-intercept. That refers to the point at which the line crosses (or "intercepts") the *y* axis (the vertical axis). We can refer to that point generically as (0, *b*). The *x* value is 0, because the point is on the *y* axis. Any point on the *y* axis has an *x* value of 0. The variable *b* in this case just represents the value of *y* where the line crosses the *y* axis. In the case of our example line, that value is -4 (see Figure 8.17). Now back to our point-slope equation.

Figure 8.17

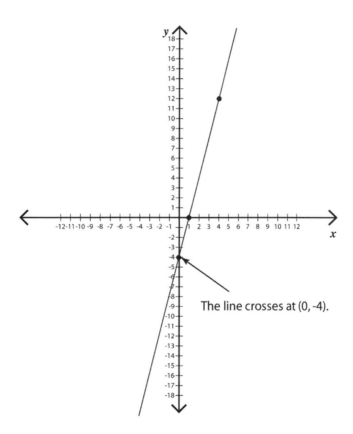

The line crosses at (0, -4).

Guidepost Using the point-slope equation of a line to derive the slope-intercept equation of a line.

The coordinate (x_1, y_1) can be *any* point on the line (remember, we chose it arbitrarily), so why not let it be the *y*-intercept? Of course we want a general equation, so instead of using the specific point (0, -4) that applies to our sample line, we'll use (0, *b*) so it applies to any line. The point-slope equation then becomes

$y - y_1 = m(x - x_1)$

$y - b = m(x - 0)$ substituting (0, *b*) for (x_1, y_1)

$y - b = mx$ because $x - 0$ is equal to x

$y - b + b = mx + b$ adding *b* to both sides of the equation

$y = mx + b$ because $-b + b$ is equal to zero

And $y = mx + b$ is the general form of the slope-intercept equation of a line. Once again, this equation comes to us via the definition of the slope of a line. The point-slope form and the *y*-intercept form of the equation of a line are not different things to memorize. They really give you the same kind of information. Just to be complete, let's figure out the slope-intercept form for our example. The slope of our line is 4, and the *y*-intercept is the point (0, -4). Therefore the slope-intercept form of the equation is

$y = mx + b$

$y = 4x + (-4)$ or $y = 4x - 4$

Chapter Summary

- Many math equations express the relationship between the dependent variable and one or more independent variables. The dependent variable "depends" on the independent variable and is usually plotted on the vertical axis of a graph.

- A function in math is a relationship in which there is only one value of the dependent variable for each value of the independent variable(s).

- The slope of a line is the rise, or the difference in *y* values, divided by the run, or the difference in corresponding *x* values. If a line slopes upward as you move to the right, the slope is positive. If a line slopes downward as you move to the right, the slope is negative.

- Using the definition of slope, you can derive two common forms of the equation of a line—the point-slope form and the *y*-intercept form.

Applications

1. Did you know that slope is a safety issue? For roads, the slope of the road is called its *grade*. A road with a 3% grade rises or drops 3 meters for each hundred meters traveled horizontally (that's just rise over run). Now, 3% might seem like a small number, but roads that have a 5% or steeper grade have warning signs posted. Lose your brakes on a 6% grade and you'd better be looking for one of those runaway truck ramps.* Railroads also take careful note of the grade of the rails. Freight trains generally are restricted to grades that are 2% or less, and passenger trains generally are restricted to grades that are 4% or less. There are standards for the slope of roofs on houses, and there is even a safety standard for how steep a slope one can navigate with a tractor.

2. Figure 8.18 shows a graph of the distance a car travels versus the time of travel. You can see that the distance steadily increases, stays the same for a while, and then increases again.

Figure 8.18

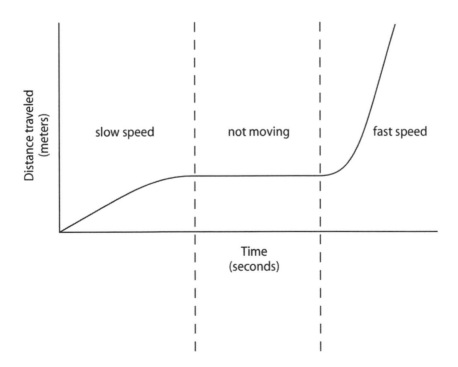

_____

* I'm sure I'm not the only one who harbors a secret desire to pick up speed and use a runaway truck ramp just to see what it's like!

Can we get more information out of this graph than the distance the car travels? Sure we can. The relationship between distance and time is given by *distance = rate · time*, or $d = rt$. Compare this to the slope-intercept equation of a line, which is $y = mx + b$. In our case, d takes the place of y, t takes the place of x, r takes the place of m, and b is equal to 0. Since m is the slope of the line in the slope-intercept form, this tells us that the slope of the graph in Figure 8.18 will always tell us the rate, or speed, at which the car is traveling. So, for the first section, the slope is gradual and the speed of the car is relatively slow. For the second section, the slope is zero (there is zero rise, so $\frac{rise}{run}$ equals 0) and the speed of the car is zero, meaning the car is at rest. In the third section, the slope is steep, meaning the speed of the car is relatively fast.

We already know the relationship between distance, rate, and time, so using a graph of values to determine rate (or speed) is sort of an academic exercise. Often in science, though, we don't know the exact mathematical relationship between quantities. If we can get experimental data and graph them, that graph can give us insight into the nature of the mathematical relationship. In fact, graphing data is one of the first steps a scientist takes when trying to figure out a new situation.

3. One example where scientists graphed a couple of quantities in order to gain insight into what's going on comes from astronomy. There are ways of measuring the luminosity (the brightness) of stars and there are ways of measuring the temperature of stars. It would seem to make sense that there would be a definite relationship between these two quantities. One way to discover this would be to graph one quantity against the other. There's a problem, though. While the range of temperatures of stars is relatively small, the range of luminosities is quite large. There are stars that have a luminosity that is $\frac{1}{10,000}$ the luminosity of the sun and there are stars that are 1,000,000 times the luminosity of the sun. How can you show such a large range of values on one graph? Logarithms to the rescue. I introduced logarithms back in the Applications section of Chapter 1, so you might want to go back and review that. Anyway, the logarithm of 10 is 1, the logarithm of 100 is 2, the logarithm of 1000 is 3, and so on. If you plot the logarithm of exponentially increasing numbers, the logarithms are evenly spaced. This allows you to plot a wide range of values in a reasonably sized graph. Figure 8.19 shows the Hertzprung-Russell diagram, which is that graph of luminosity (brightness) versus temperature of stars I told you about. On the vertical axis, the luminosities are listed as $L_\odot$, $10,000L_\odot$, $\frac{1}{1,000}L_\odot$, etc. $L_\odot$ refers to the luminosity of our sun, so that the luminosities of all other stars are plotted in relation to the sun's luminosity. Notice that the luminosity is graphed

using a logarithmic scale, so that even though the luminosity increases exponentially, the markings are evenly spaced. The labels on the vertical axis don't indicate logarithms, but that's what they are. If the luminosities were plotted directly, the mark indicating $10,000L_\odot$ would be 100 times farther from the mark $L_\odot$ than is the mark $100L_\odot$.

It's a bit too complicated to go into here, but the Hertzsprung-Russell diagram gives astronomers lots and lots of information not just about how luminosity is related to temperature, but about how stars evolve, from birth to death.

Figure 8.19

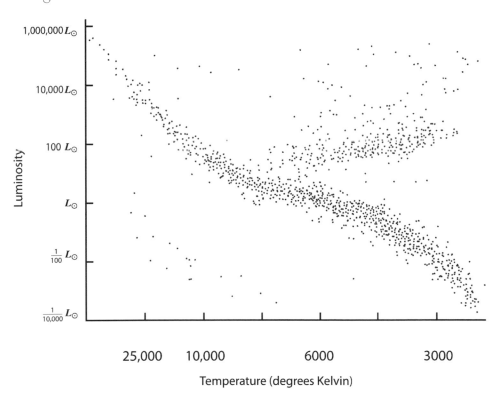

Pie Are Not Round; πr^2

What would a math book be without a nerdy math joke? Bad jokes aside, you might recognize πr^2 as the formula for the area of a circle. And you might infer from that fact that this chapter addresses geometry. Often people think of geometry as a bunch of formulas for finding the area of objects, the volume of objects, and the distance around various shapes. In addition, there are methods for determining how angles and lengths of sides help you make conclusions about the shape of things, and on and on. Unfortunately, that approach alone doesn't lead to a lot of understanding. Back when I taught college physics, various area and volume formulas entered the picture. I used to ask the students why the area of a rectangle is the length times the width, and why the area of a circle is πr^2. Usually at least half the class had absolutely

"I could remember pi to the 100th place, but I couldn't remember our anniversary."

no idea, other than these being the correct formulas. Here's hoping you don't leave this chapter without knowing this and more.

Things to do before you read the explanation

Figure 9.1

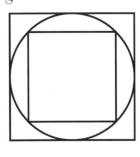

Figure 9.1 shows a circle and its diameter. Use a ruler to measure the length of the diameter in centimeters.

Figure 9.2 shows a series of drawings of this same circle. This time, however, there are different shapes drawn inside and outside the circle.

For each drawing, measure the distance all the way around (this is known as the **perimeter**, by the way) both the inside and outside shapes. As the segments of the figures get smaller and smaller, it's harder to get an accurate measurement, but do the best you can. Keep track of the numbers you get. Do the inside perimeters and outside perimeters get closer to each other as you progress through the drawings? Of course they do. By the time you get to the last drawing, those two perimeters should be pretty close in value. Choose a number about halfway between the final inside and outside perimeters and divide that number by the length of the diameter of the circle. What number do you get? Why in the world am I having you do this? Read on and see.

Figure 9.2

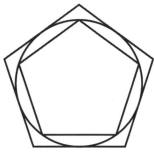

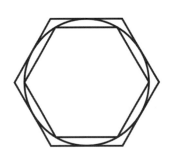

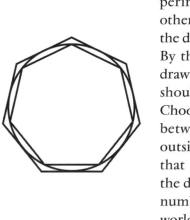

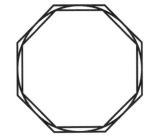

The explanation

Beginning thousands of years ago, philosophers[*] were fascinated with various shapes such as circles and triangles. Yes, maybe they needed to get a social life, but they discovered remarkable things about those shapes. One thing they discovered was that if you measured the distance around a circle and divided it by the circle's diameter, you ended up with a number that was pretty much the same, regardless of the size of the circle. For people who were taken by the circular shape as some kind of perfection, this was a big deal. In fact, it's a big deal today. It has everything to do with that special number π (pronounced "pie") that we use so often in geometry. Try as they might, those philosophers couldn't come up with an exact number for the circumference of a circle divided by its diameter, and we still can't today.

Why can't you get an exact number for π? Part of the answer has to do with the fact that you cannot accurately measure the distance around a circle (its circumference) directly. You can accurately measure the length of a section of line, but since a circle continuously changes direction, there are no straight segments to measure. You can break up the circle into many tiny straight sections, but that will only be an approximation of the circle. Any direct measure of the distance around a circle is therefore only an approximation.

Here's where the activity I had you do comes in. With each successive drawing, the figures drawn inside and outside the circle more closely approximated the circle itself. So, choosing a number about halfway in between the perimeter of the outside and inside figures in the final drawing might be a good estimate of the circumference of the circle. Then dividing that number by the diameter should give you a reasonable estimate of π. Aristotle did something quite similar to the activity you did in order to determine the value of π. He measured the areas of the figures rather than their perimeters, but the general idea was the same. Aristotle was your basic dedicated philosopher, as he used 96-sided figures to make his approximation. Today, mathematicians use many different methods to calculate π, many of them involving adding and subtracting infinite series of fractions or probability techniques. Of course, you can never get an exact number for π because it's an **irrational number**, meaning that it can be carried out to an infinite number of decimal places without ever repeating. To five decimal places, π is equal to 3.14159... [†]

---

[*] In the early days of civilization, philosophers didn't just do what philosophers today do. They studied math and science along with figuring out humans' place in the universe and all that. Early philosophers *were* the scientists and mathematicians of their day.

[†] I had a housemate in graduate school who had memorized π to 100 decimal places. They did such things at MIT, where he was an undergraduate.

Guidepost Explaining how one can approximate a value for π.

The method you used, and the method Aristotle used, for calculating π is known as calculating a **limit**. We can't measure the circumference of a circle directly, but we can slowly approach that limit by making better and better approximations of the measurement we want. The concept of a limit is really important in calculus, which I'll address in the final chapter.

More things to do before you read more explanation

Figure 9.3 shows a whole bunch of squares, each measuring one centimeter on a side.

Make a copy of Figure 9.3 and then cut out each individual square. Then find out how many of these squares fit inside each of the shapes in Figure 9.4. If you can't determine that exactly, then do your best to estimate.

Figure 9.3

Figure 9.4

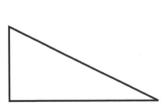

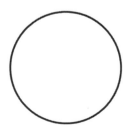

More explanation

You just tried to fit squares that are 1 centimeter on a side inside various shapes. This process illustrates what the term *area* means. The area of a shape is simply how much "two-dimensional space" there is inside the shape. A simple way to determine the area of something is to find out how many 1-centimeter squares fit inside that shape. If six of those squares fit inside the shape, then the area of that shape is 6 square centimeters, or 6 cm². (I should note here that cm is the abbreviation for centimeters.) The rectangle was easy to figure out. Eight squares fit neatly inside that shape, so its area is 8 square centimeters. Also, because there are two rows with four squares each, you can see why the area of a rectangle is equal to its length times its width, or $A = lw$, with l being the length and w being the width. See Figure 9.5.

Figure 9.5

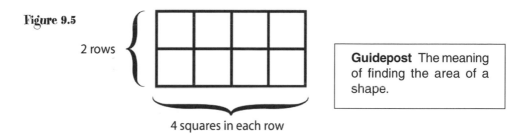

2 rows

4 squares in each row

> **Guidepost** The meaning of finding the area of a shape.

Figuring out the area of a parallelogram (the shape in the upper right of Figure 9.4), circle, or triangle isn't so easy. For one thing, the centimeter squares do not fit neatly inside the shape. So, determining the area by placing squares in the shape means you have to estimate the result. What we do is try to be clever and figure out formulas that will help us determine the area of a shape other than a rectangle. We'll work on the parallelogram in the next section.

Even more things to do before you read more explanation

I'm going to begin this section by giving you a formula for the area of a parallelogram, so named because the opposite sides of the shape are parallel and also the same length. See Figure 9.6.

To determine the area of a parallelogram, you use the formula $A = bh$, where A is the area, b is the length of the base, and h is the height,

Figure 9.6

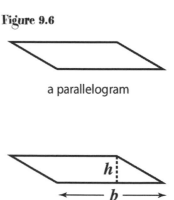

a parallelogram

Area $= bh$

shown in the second diagram in Figure 9.6. To determine the height, you simply drop a line from the top side of the parallelogram down to the base. This line should be perpendicular (making an angle of 90 degrees) with the base. Now, let's say our parallelogram has the measurements shown in Figure 9.7. Figure out the area of this parallelogram.

Figure 9.7

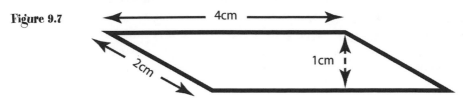

If you got an answer of 4 square centimeters, then you used the formula correctly. Now for your challenge. Figure 9.8 shows another parallelogram. Using the formula for the area of a parallelogram, $A = bh$, find the area of this parallelogram.

Figure 9.8

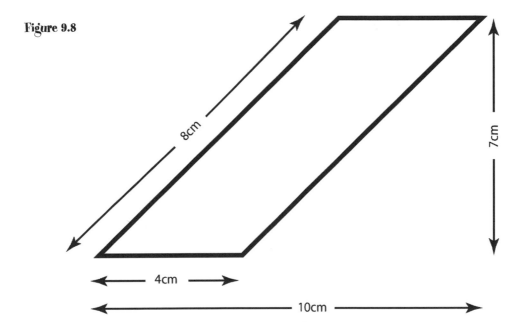

Even more explanation

I started out the previous section asking you to do what I generally preach not to do, which is take a formula and just apply it without knowing where the formula comes from. I did that to make a point. This is an example provided by psychologist Max Wertheimer, who was one of the pioneers of a movement known as Gestalt psychology that sprang up around 1930. As the story goes, he was observing an elementary school classroom, where students were learning the formula for calculating the area of a parallelogram. All the examples were like the first drawing in Figure 9.6. He then asked the teacher if he could ask the students a question, whereupon he produced the parallelogram in Figure 9.8. Although some students had no problem with the new task, many got completely confused. Wertheimer reports that students produced drawings similar to those in Figure 9.9, in an attempt to apply the formula for area. Maybe you did the same kind of thing, but maybe not. The whole point is that using a memorized formula can often lead to confusion. More on this example later in this section.

Figure 9.9

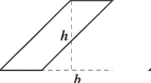 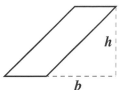

Of course, you already know the formula for the area of a parallelogram, so let's see if we can make that formula make sense. The key is to realize that you can transform a parallelogram into a rectangle by removing a triangle from one end and placing it on the other end, as in Figure 9.10. Now it's clear why the formula for the area of a parallelogram is $A = bh$.

Figure 9.10

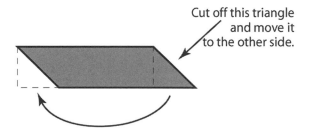

Cut off this triangle and move it to the other side.

> **Guidepost** The reasoning behind the formula for the area of a parallelogram.

Our friend Wertheimer claimed that if the students he worked with had had a basic understanding of what area means, and had been exposed to the reasoning behind the formula for the area of a rectangle and other shapes, then they would have been able to solve the problem he posed when he asked about a parallelogram that wasn't in the "normal" orientation.

Now you have a rectangle with area **bh.**

Let's move on to finding the area of a triangle. Once again, you have a shape in which centimeter squares don't fit easily. You have to estimate the answer. On the other hand, we can be clever to figure out the proper formula for the area of a triangle. No matter what size or shape triangle you have, you can view it as what you get when you draw a line that cuts either a rectangle or a parallelogram* in half, as in Figure 9.11.

Figure 9.11

> **Guidepost** The reasoning behind the formula for the area of a triangle.

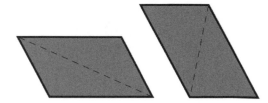

All triangles are half of a parallelogram or rectangle.

Because each triangle is obtained by cutting a rectangle or parallelogram in half, the area of a triangle is half the area of the rectangle or parallelogram. So, if the area of a parallelogram is the base times the height, then the area of the triangle is half that, or $A = \frac{1}{2}bh$. See Figure 9.12.

Finally, let's see if we can be clever enough to come up with a formula for the area of a circle. You already know that the area of a circle is πr^2, where r is the radius of the circle, but wouldn't it be nice to know where that

Figure 9.12

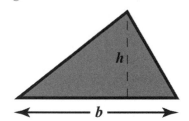

The area of this triangle is ½ bh.

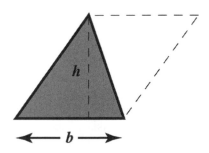

The area of the parallelogram is bh.

---

* For the record, every rectangle is just a special case of a parallelogram, one in which all angles are right angles. So, all rectangles are also parallelograms.

formula comes from? Sure it would. Figure 9.13 shows a circle and a segment of that circle.

Figure 9.13

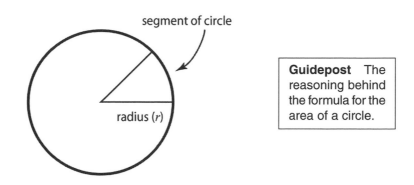

segment of circle

radius (*r*)

> **Guidepost** The reasoning behind the formula for the area of a circle.

If we knew the area of that segment, we could just add up the areas of similar segments to get the area of the circle. Unfortunately, we don't know the area of that segment. We can be tricky, though, and make that segment really, really small. If we make it small enough, then the segment comes awfully close to being a triangle. In fact, we can imagine making the segment so small that we can consider the short side to be so small that there really isn't any difference between the short side being a curved line (part of the edge of the circle) and a straight line. In other words, we can get a good approximation of the area of the segment by assuming that it *is* a triangle. See Figure 9.14.

Figure 9.14

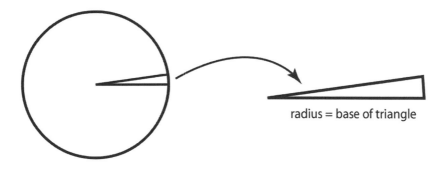

radius = base of triangle

If the segment is small enough, it's very close to being a triangle.

Now, the area of this triangle is just $\frac{1}{2}bh$, where the length of the base is just the radius of the circle. Now let's add up the areas of a whole bunch of segments that are the same size as the one we have already. Then we have the following situation, shown in Figure 9.15.

Area of entire circle = sum of the areas of the individual segments

$$= \frac{1}{2}rh_1 + \frac{1}{2}rh_2 + \frac{1}{2}rh_3 + \dots$$

Now we can use the distributive property (you remember that from Chapter 1, don't you?) to rewrite this expression as

Area of entire circle = $\frac{1}{2}r(h_1 + h_2 + h_3 + \dots)$

The expression inside the parentheses is the sum of all the h's. That sum is simply the total distance around the circle,[*] or the circumference of the circle. But we already know that value. The definition of π is the circumference of the circle divided by its diameter. Couple that with the fact that the diameter of a circle is twice its radius, and you end up with an expression for the circumference.

Figure 9.15

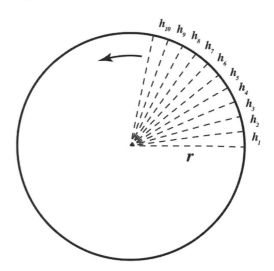

Adding the areas of the triangles gives you the area of the circle.

$$\pi = \frac{circumference}{diameter} = \frac{C}{twice\ the\ radius} = \frac{C}{2r}$$

$$\pi = \frac{C}{2r}$$

Next we can multiply both sides of this equation by $2r$.

$$2r \cdot \pi = \frac{C}{2r} \cdot 2r$$

$2\pi r = C$ \qquad rearranging the left side using the commutative property and canceling the $2r$ terms on the right

---

[*] Actually, the sum of all the h's is only approximately equal to the circumference of the circle. To get an exact answer, we have to imagine going to the *limit* of this sum as each h gets closer and closer to having zero height.

So, the circumference of a circle is $2\pi r$. Now we can go back to our expression for the area of the circle, which is

Area of entire circle = $\frac{1}{2}r(h_1 + h_2 + h_3 + ...)$

Area of entire circle = $\frac{1}{2}r(2\pi r)$ substituting $2\pi r$ for the circumference

Area of entire circle = πr^2 canceling the 2s and multiplying the r's to get r^2

You might think I cheated just a bit with the technique I used. I mean, you really can't make a segment of a circle so small that it actually *is* a triangle, can you? Nope, but you can imagine doing it. In the *limit* of an infinitesimally small segment, that segment becomes a triangle (with a height of zero, of course!). To do this properly, then, we would have to use calculus, but the idea is the same.

And even more things to do before reading even more explanation

The top drawing in Figure 9.16 shows a right triangle (so named because one of the angles is a right angle of 90 degrees) drawn on top of a pattern of tiles. The drawing below it in Figure 9.16 shows the same triangle sharing its sides with different squares. See if you can use this drawing to verify the Pythagorean Theorem, which is that $a^2 + b^2 = c^2$, where a, b, and c are the lengths of the sides of the triangle.

Figure 9.16

Guidepost Verification of the Pythagorean Theorem.

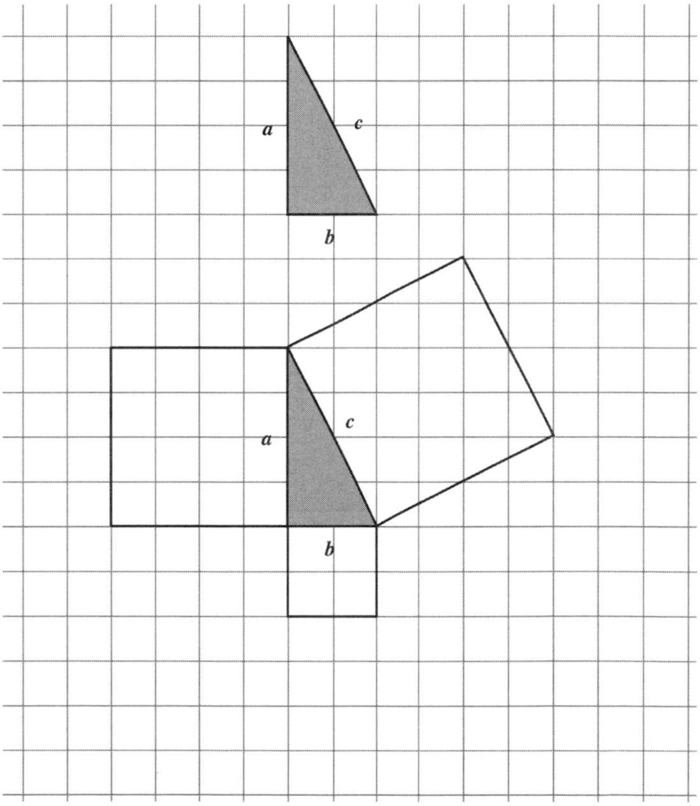

More fun with triangles. The first drawing in Figure 9.17 shows our triangle drawn inside a circle, so that the length of the side *c* is equal to the radius of the circle. Notice that this circle is drawn on top of a set of *x* and *y* axes, with *x* = 0, *y* = 0 being at the center of the circle. Also note that there are positive and negative values of *x* and *y*. The rest of the drawings in Figure 9.17 show what happens to the triangle as the radius moves counterclockwise around the circle. Notice that as this happens, the numbers that represent *a* and *b* go through positive and negative values.

Figure 9.17

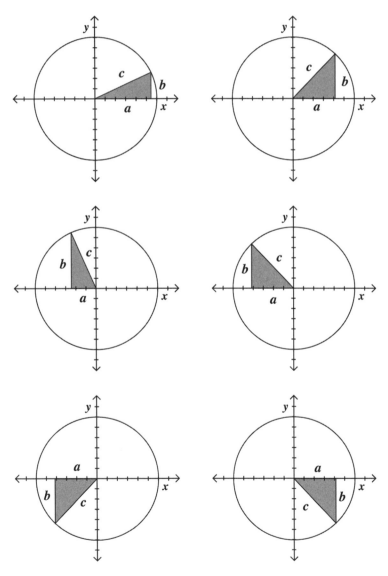

Here's your task. Calculate the value of the fraction $\frac{a}{c}$ and the fraction $\frac{b}{c}$ for the various drawings. These don't have to be exact. Do remember that a and b can be both positive and negative. Keep the value of c, though, as always being positive, so c is always equal to 6. In case that just confused you, I'll do the calculation for the fourth drawing. In that drawing, a is about -4 (it's negative because it's to the left of zero on the x axis) and b is about 5 (it's positive because it's above zero on the y axis). Therefore, $\frac{a}{c}$ equals $-\frac{4}{6}$ and $\frac{b}{c}$ equals $\frac{5}{6}$.

Once you make those calculations, take a more general look at the quantities $\frac{a}{c}$ and $\frac{b}{c}$. What is the maximum value that each of these can have? What is the minimum value of each? Yes, I'll explain why in the world you're doing this in the next section.

Even more explanation

In addition to being fascinated with shapes such as circles and rectangles, early philosophers were taken with triangles, so much so that the study of triangles has its own name—trigonometry. One of the most famous results of trigonometry is the Pythagorean Theorem, or $a^2 + b^2 = c^2$, where a, b, and c are the sides of a right triangle. Did you figure out how to verify this using Figure 9.16? If not, here's how you do it. You can determine the area of each square in that second drawing by counting up the number of smaller squares and/or triangles inside the large squares. There are four small squares in one of the smaller large squares, 16 small squares in the other smaller large square, and 20 small squares in the large square. That means that the area of the large square is equal to the sum of the areas of the smaller squares. Now, a square is just a special case of a rectangle, so the area of a square is its length times its width. Since the length of a square is equal to its width, then the area of a square is the length of one side squared. So, we have

(area of one small square) + (area of the other small square) =
area of large square

$$a^2 + b^2 = c^2$$

And that's the Pythagorean Theorem. You read it as "the square of the hypotenuse (the hypotenuse is the longest side of the triangle) is equal to the sum of the squares of the other two sides."

On to those silly measurements I had you make on the triangles. First I have to define two functions that you might have heard of. Those functions are the sine function and the cosine function. You might not have thought of these two things as functions before. Rather you probably know them as being defined as measurements on a right triangle. The sine of an angle is defined as the length of the opposite side divided by the length of the hypotenuse (the longest side) and the cosine of an angle is defined as the length of the adjacent side divided by the length of the hypotenuse. See Figure 9.18, and notice that the angle is labeled with the Greek letter "theta," written as θ.

Figure 9.18

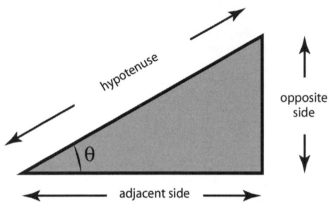

The definition of sine and cosine in terms of a right triangle are useful all by themselves. You can use them, along with a third function known as the tangent,* to figure out all sorts of geometric relationships. I want to focus on their value as mathematical functions, though, which brings us to your measurements of $\frac{a}{c}$ and $\frac{b}{c}$ as the right triangles moved around the circle counterclockwise. Given our definitions of sine and cosine, maybe you now know that what you were calculating was the sine and cosine functions as you moved counterclockwise around the circle. You should have found that the values of the sine and cosine could both be negative or positive, but that they never got larger than 1 or smaller than -1. Figure 9.19 shows a few critical points and the values of the sine and cosine functions at those points.

Guidepost Definition of the sine and cosine functions.

---

* The tangent is defined as the length of the opposite side divided by the length of the adjacent side.

Figure 9.19

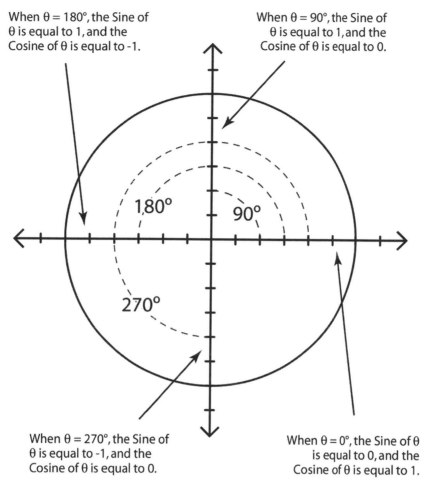

When θ = 180°, the Sine of θ is equal to 1, and the Cosine of θ is equal to -1.

When θ = 90°, the Sine of θ is equal to 1, and the Cosine of θ is equal to 0.

180°

90°

270°

When θ = 270°, the Sine of θ is equal to -1, and the Cosine of θ is equal to 0.

When θ = 0°, the Sine of θ is equal to 0, and the Cosine of θ is equal to 1.

Maybe you can imagine that the values of the sine and cosine change smoothly as you move slowly around the circle, going between a maximum of +1 and a minimum of -1. In fact, we can graph these functions, using the relationships $y = \sin(\theta)$ and $y = \cos(\theta)$.* Those graphs are shown in Figure 9.20 on the next page. You might check that these are indeed functions because for each value of θ, there is only one unique value of y.

---

* The abbreviations for sine and cosine are sin and cos. So, $\sin(\theta)$ means to take the sine of the angle θ, and $\cos(\theta)$ means to take the cosine of the angle θ. Also, sin θ and $\sin(\theta)$ mean the same thing, as do cos θ and $\cos(\theta)$.

Figure 9.20

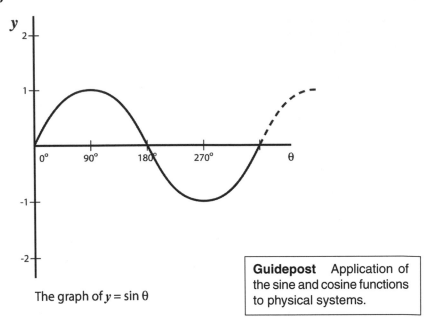

The graph of $y = \sin \theta$

> **Guidepost** Application of the sine and cosine functions to physical systems.

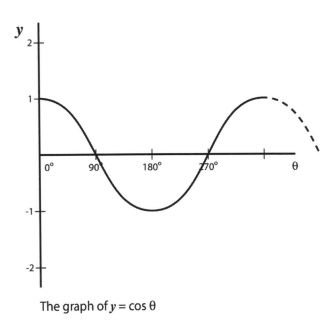

The graph of $y = \cos \theta$

Being a mind reader, I can tell that many of you are thinking, "So what? Isn't this just the kind of abstract math that you said you weren't going to do in this book?" Well, here's the connection to reality. Many physical systems oscillate back and forth between a maximum and a minimum. One example is a pendulum, which is just a weight on a string that moves back and forth. Another is a weight attached to a spring, which moves up and down between a maximum and a minimum. Figure 9.21 shows both of these.

More abstract examples of things that oscillate back and forth between extremes are waves on a string, models of light waves, and models of sound waves. All of these things can be described mathematically with the sine and cosine functions, meaning these functions are powerful things in science.

Well, there are many more things in geometry that I could discuss, but as with the rest of this book, I can't do it all without this becoming a textbook. A bit more on this topic appears in the Applications section and in the next chapter.

Figure 9.21

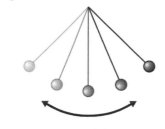

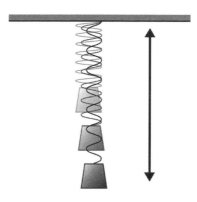

a pendulum

a mass on a spring

"I prefer to think of it as an oscillating physical system. Not a weight problem."

Chapter Summary

- To find the area of an object, you must determine how many square centimeters, square meters, square inches, or the like fit inside the object.

- Finding the area of an object often involves figuring out how the shape of the object is related to the shape of a simpler object.

- The number represented by the letter π is defined as the circumference (distance around) of a circle divided by the diameter (distance across) of the circle. It is impossible to determine an exact number for π.

- The Pythagorean Theorem applies to right triangles (triangles with an angle of 90 degrees) and states that the sum of the squares of the lengths of the shorter sides is equal to the square of the length of the longest side. You can verify the Pythagorean Theorem by using extra squares drawn around a right triangle.

- The sine of an angle is equal to the length of the opposite side divided by the length of the hypotenuse of a right triangle that contains the angle.

- The cosine of an angle is equal to the length of the adjacent side divided by the length of the hypotenuse of a right triangle that contains the angle.

- The sine and cosine functions vary smoothly and describe many physical systems that oscillate back and forth.

Applications

1. A trapezoid is a four-sided figure that has only two sides that are parallel. Figure 9.22 shows a trapezoid.

Figure 9.22

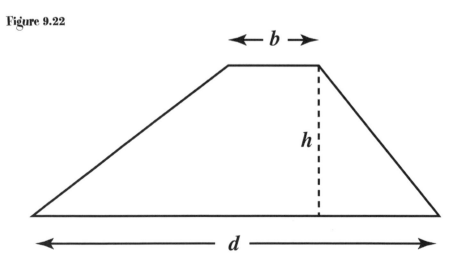

The formula for the area of a trapezoid is $A = \frac{1}{2}h(d+b)$. Let's see if we can make sense of that. In Figure 9.23, I have drawn an extra line on the trapezoid.

This line makes it clear that you can separate the trapezoid into a rectangle with sides b and h, and two triangles on either end. We can combine those two triangles on the ends into one triangle that has a base of length $d - b$, and a height of h. The area of this triangle is $\frac{1}{2}h(d-b)$, and the area of the rectangle is bh. So, to get the total area of the trapezoid, we have to add the area of the triangle and the area of the rectangle.

Figure 9.23

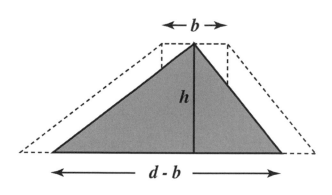

A rectangle of width b and height h.

The two triangles left over combine to make one triangle.

area of trapezoid = area of triangle + area of rectangle

$$= \frac{1}{2}h(d-b) + bh$$

$$= \frac{1}{2}hd - \frac{1}{2}hb + bh \quad \text{used the distributive property}$$
on the left term

$$= \frac{1}{2}hd + (-\frac{1}{2}hb) + hb \quad \text{rewrote the minus as "plus a negative"}$$
and changed the order of b and h in
the last term (commutative property)

$$= \frac{1}{2}hd + \frac{1}{2}hb \quad \text{because } (-\frac{1}{2}hb) + hb \text{ is equal to } \frac{1}{2}hb$$

$$= \frac{1}{2}h(d+b) \quad \text{used the distributive property in reverse.}$$

And that's the original formula for the area of a trapezoid. To recap, I broke up the figure into a rectangle and two triangles and combined the two triangles into one triangle. Then I found the areas of those figures separately, added them together, and simplified the final answer.

2. When you study trigonometry, you learn all sorts of "trig identities" that describe the relationships between various functions of angles, such as sines, cosines, tangents, secants, cotangents, and on and on. One of the first identities you encounter is the following:

$$\sin^2\theta + \cos^2\theta = 1$$

No, we're not going to use that identity here, but we can easily show where it comes from. First, you have to remember the definitions of the sine and cosine. Figure 9.24 shows a right triangle with sides a, b, and c, along with the angle θ. The sine of this angle is the length of the opposite side, b, divided by the length of the hypotenuse, c. The cosine of this angle is the length of the adjacent side, a, divided by the length of the hypotenuse, c. So, $\sin\theta = \frac{b}{c}$ and $\cos\theta = \frac{a}{c}$.

Figure 9.24

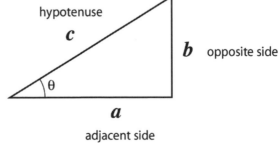

hypotenuse

c

b opposite side

θ

a

adjacent side

Because this triangle is a right triangle, we know that the Pythagorean Theorem applies, meaning that

$a^2 + b^2 = c^2$

I'm going to divide both sides of this equation by c^2 to get

$$\frac{a^2+b^2}{c^2} = \frac{c^2}{c^2}$$

Next I'm going to use the distributive property to simplify the left-hand side. I could do that directly by dividing both a^2 and b^2 by c^2, but we haven't used the distributive property with division much, so I'm going to rewrite division by c^2 as a multiplication by $\frac{1}{c^2}$ (division is the same as multiplying by the reciprocal, and vice versa—see Chapter 3).

$$\frac{1}{c^2}(a^2+b^2) = \frac{c^2}{c^2}$$

Next I'll just use the distributive property on the left side and realize that $\frac{c^2}{c^2}$ is equal to 1 on the right side.

$$\frac{1}{c^2} \cdot a^2 + \frac{1}{c^2} \cdot b^2 = \frac{c^2}{c^2}$$

$$\frac{1}{c^2} \cdot a^2 + \frac{1}{c^2} \cdot b^2 = 1$$

Now I'll change those multiplications back to divisions, using what we know about reciprocals.

$$\frac{a^2}{c^2} + \frac{b^2}{c^2} = 1$$

We're almost there. The next thing to realize is that $\frac{a^2}{c^2}$ is equal to $\left(\frac{a}{c}\right)^2$ and $\frac{b^2}{c^2}$ is equal to $\left(\frac{b}{c}\right)^2$. If you don't see why those are true, try writing a^2 as $a \cdot a$, b^2 as $b \cdot b$, and c^2 as $c \cdot c$. You should be able to figure it out. Anyway, what we now have is

$$\left(\frac{a}{c}\right)^2 + \left(\frac{b}{c}\right)^2 = 1$$

But we have different names for $\frac{a}{c}$ and $\frac{b}{c}$. They're $\cos\theta$ and $\sin\theta$. Therefore, we have

$(\cos\theta)^2 + (\sin\theta)^2 = 1$

It's conventional to write the squares of trig functions slightly differently from this, so the final result is usually written as

$\sin^2\theta + \cos^2\theta = 1$

Okay, why is it important for you to see how one comes up with this trig identity? Well, it's *not* all that important in terms of this particular result. The point is that all those complicated-looking expressions in trigonometry are based on relatively simple ideas. It might take a number of math steps to get to a particular result, but each step in the process makes sense, just like everything else in math.

Not So Scary Calculus

Given that the vast majority of people reading this book will never ever have to teach calculus, you might be wondering why in the world I'm addressing the topic. Well, even though you might not teach calculus, chances are that when teaching math and science you are using results that come from the application of calculus. When Junior asks where in the world the formula for the volume of a sphere comes from, you can go beyond saying, "It's calculus, Junior," to giving Junior a rough idea of the processes involved in finding that formula. So no, I'm not going to teach you to do calculus, but rather to understand the basic concepts upon which calculus is based. Those basic concepts are surprisingly simple, even though the calculations in calculus can get downright intimidating. Suffice to say we won't get into those intimidating calculations here.

While testing the limits of calculus, Tammy also tested the patience of her father.

Things to do before you read the explanation

Stand about 2 meters away from a wall, facing the wall. Take a step so that the toe of your shoe (or your actual toe if barefoot) covers half the distance between you and the wall. Then take a step so the toe of your shoe covers half the remaining distance. Then take a step so the toe of your shoe covers half the remaining distance again. Keep doing this until you can no longer take small enough steps to cover only half the remaining distance between you and the wall. Is the toe of your foot touching the wall? If you were able to keep taking smaller and smaller steps, each time covering half the remaining distance with the toe of your shoe, would you ever reach the wall?

Here's something similar to walking toward a wall, even though the connection might not be obvious right away. Figure 10.1 shows the graph of the function $y = 1 + \dfrac{1}{x}$.

Figure 10.1

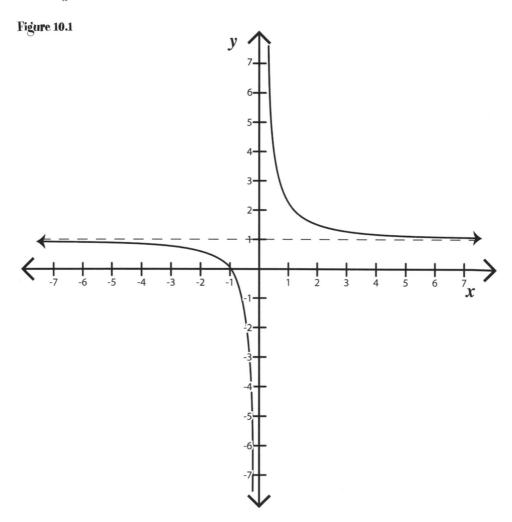

As x gets larger and larger positively and negatively, $\frac{1}{x}$ gets smaller and smaller (the fraction gets smaller) and y gets closer and closer to a value of 1. You can see this both in the graph and just by looking at the function. Does y ever actually equal 1?

One more situation to consider. You can calculate the average speed of something using the relationship $speed = \frac{\text{distance traveled}}{\text{time to travel that distance}}$.* That's relatively easy to calculate whether the distance traveled is short or long. But what if you want the *instantaneous* speed of something, meaning the speed it is traveling at one instant of time? In a single instant of time, the object doesn't travel *any* distance! Does that mean the speed at that instant is zero, since the distance traveled is zero? Clearly not. Does this mean you can't use the above relationship?

The explanation

In walking toward a wall and covering half the remaining distance each time, you will never actually reach the wall. Of course, you can get as close to the wall as you want just by taking more steps. As the number of steps gets larger and larger, approaching an infinite number of steps, you can say that for all practical purposes, you *are* at the wall. In other words, the limit of your motion as the number of steps gets arbitrarily large is that you are touching the wall.

Guidepost The concept of a limit.

Refer to Figure 10.1. In that graph, the value of y never actually equals 1, but it *approaches* the value of 1 as x gets larger and larger. You could say that the *limit* of the value of y is equal to 1 as the value of x approaches infinity. Of course, you can never get to infinity, so y is never equal to 1, but we can imagine that process.

We have a similar situation with calculating instantaneous speed. You can calculate the speed of an object for a short time period near the time you're interested in. The object moves a short distance in that short time. Then you can make the time period and distance moved shorter and shorter, getting as close as you want to zero distance traveled in zero time. For most everyday situations, you will find that the speed you calculate gets closer and closer to a specific number—the *limit* of your calculations. See Figure 10.2.

---

* See the *Stop Faking It!* book on Force and Motion for a detailed discussion of speed.

Figure 10.2

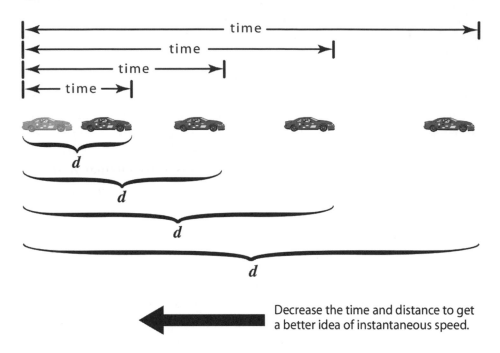

Decrease the time and distance to get a better idea of instantaneous speed.

Chapter 9 contained two more examples of limits. The first was in calculating a value for π by using the perimeter of many-sided shapes drawn inside and outside a circle (Figure 9.2). As those shapes increased the number of sides, their perimeters got closer and closer to the perimeter (circumference) of the circle. We can say that the limit of the perimeter of the shapes, as the number of sides approaches infinity, is the perimeter of the circle. The second example of a limit in Chapter 9 was the derivation of a formula for the area of a circle. I asked you to imagine smaller and smaller segments of the circle. In the limit as the size of the segments approaches zero, the segments approach being right triangles. Refer back to Figures 9.14 and 9.15.

The reason I'm spending so much time on limits is that this concept is the cornerstone of calculus. Behind each strange-looking symbol and complicated-looking series of equations in calculus is the basic idea of using limits to get results.

More things to do before you read more explanation

The graph in Figure 10.3 should serve as a reminder of how to calculate the slope of a line. You simply choose two points on the line and then divide the difference in the *y* values by the difference in the *x* values (this is the rise divided by the run).[*]

Figure 10.3

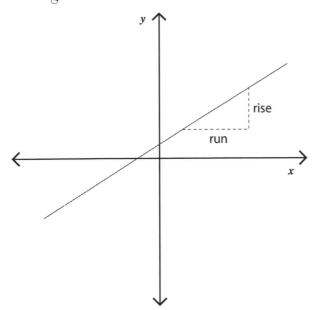

Figure 10.4 shows a different situation, where the graph is curved. I've shown a few dotted lines that you *might* use to determine rise over run.

There isn't just one slope for this graph, as the slope is constantly changing. In fact, those rise over run dotted lines in Figure 10.4 are clearly incorrect, as the segment of the graph encompassed in each is not a straight line. See if you can come up with a method for finding the slope of this graph at any particular point.

> **Guidepost** How do you find the slope of a line if the slope keeps changing?

Figure 10.4

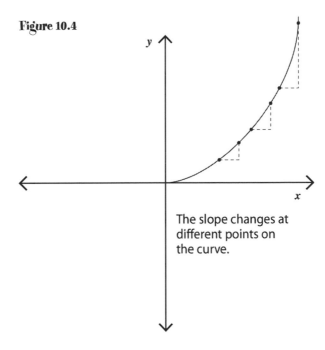

The slope changes at different points on the curve.

---

[*] Remember that, in the case of a line that slopes downward as you go to the right, the "rise" is actually negative, leading to a negative slope. Not the case here, but worth a reminder.

More explanation

One possible way to figure out the slope of this graph at one particular point is to draw a line that is parallel to the direction the graph slopes at that point. Such a line is known as the tangent to the graph at that point.[*] Unfortunately, you can only get an accurate slope if you draw an exact line and make great measurements. It would be nice to get an answer that doesn't require any measurements. We have the same situation as when you want to calculate the instantaneous speed of something. It's impossible to calculate the slope of the graph at one point using $\frac{rise}{run}$ because at a single point, the rise and the run are both zero. So, what you do is calculate the rise over run for two points that get closer and closer together, approaching the point of interest, and figure out the limit of the value of rise over run. Figure 10.5 shows this process. The point A remains in one spot, and the point B moves closer and closer to point A.

Figure 10.5

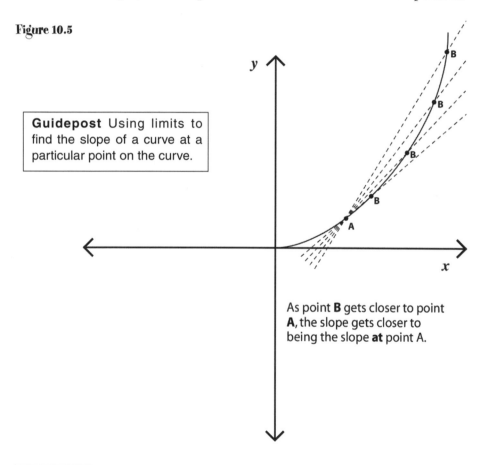

> **Guidepost** Using limits to find the slope of a curve at a particular point on the curve.

As point **B** gets closer to point **A**, the slope gets closer to being the slope **at** point A.

---

[*] This is not the same as the trigonometric function of tangent I talked about in the Applications section of Chapter 9.

There's a special name for the process of finding the limit of the change in one thing divided by the change in another. It's called finding the derivative. It even has a special notation. The derivative that represents the limit of the change in y over the change in x (this is rise over run) is $\frac{dy}{dx}$. As one example, let's calculate the derivative of the function $y = x^2$, the graph of which is shown in Figure 10.6.

Figure 10.6

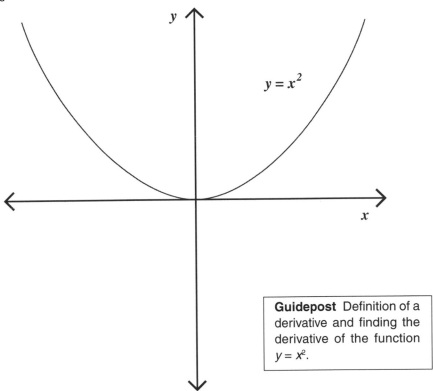

$y = x^2$

> **Guidepost** Definition of a derivative and finding the derivative of the function $y = x^2$.

What we want is the limit of $\frac{y_2 - y_1}{x_2 - x_1}$ as $x_2 - x_1$ approaches zero. To figure that out, we need to substitute a value of x^2 for each of our y values. Then the expression we want the limit of becomes $\frac{x_2^2 - x_1^2}{x_2 - x_1}$. Before going on, note that at the limit, $x_2 - x_1$ is equal to zero. We can't just put a 0 in for $x_2 - x_1$ because then we would be dividing by zero. That's a big no-no in math, and is termed "undefined." We can work around that, though. We can rewrite $x_2^2 - x_1^2$ as $(x_2 + x_1)(x_2 - x_1)$. In case that's not obvious to you, you can do the multiplication. Two of the terms in that multiplication add to zero, and you're left with $x_2^2 - x_1^2$. So now we have

$$\frac{x_2^2 - x_1^2}{x_2 - x_1} = \frac{(x_2 + x_1)(x_2 - x_1)}{x_2 - x_1}$$

Remember, we want the limit of this last expression as $x_2 - x_1$ approaches zero. We can't actually go to that limit yet, because again we would be dividing by zero. Fortunately for us, the $x_2 - x_1$ on top of that expression cancels with the $x_2 - x_1$ on the bottom. So,

$$\frac{(x_2 + x_1)(x_2 - x_1)}{x_2 - x_1} = \frac{(x_2 + x_1)(\cancel{x_2 - x_1})}{\cancel{x_2 - x_1}} = x_2 + x_1$$

With no expression that will equal zero in the denominator, we can now go to the limit and let $x_2 - x_1$ actually equal zero, meaning that x_2 is equal to x_1. If they're equal, then we can just write $x_2 + x_1$ as $2x_1$. Because x_1 and x_2 are just arbitrary points on the graph, this expression is true for any value of x we choose. So, the derivative of the function x^2 is equal to $2x$. So who cares? Well, recall what the derivative of a graph tells us. It gives the value of the slope of the graph at any one point. That's a valuable thing to know, especially if the graph illustrates something like the distance something moves in a given amount of time. The slope of that graph is the change in distance divided by the change in time, which is just our definition of speed. So, if you have an expression that tells you the distance something travels over time, you can just take the derivative of that expression and get the speed. Much of science involves mathematical relationships between various quantities, the changes in those quantities, and even the changes in the changes of those quantities. Those relationships can be represented with various quantities and their derivatives. Neat.

Even more things to do before you read even more explanation

Figure 10.7 shows another graph of a line and illustrates how you would go about finding the area underneath that graph. For now just accept that this is something you might have a reason for doing. The area underneath the graph in Figure 10.7 is relatively easy to calculate. What you have is just a triangle, and we already know how to find the area of a triangle.

Now take a look at the graph in Figure 10.8, which is again a graph of the function $y = x^2$. The area

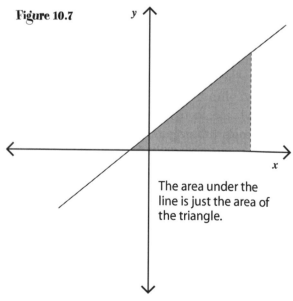

Figure 10.7

The area under the line is just the area of the triangle.

underneath this graph is shaded.

How do you suppose you would go about calculating the area that's shaded? If you need a hint, look back to Chapter 9 and see how I came up with the area of a circle. You have to do something similar here. Of course, you won't be able to actually do the calculation, so just outline the method.

Even more explanation

As I already discussed earlier in this chapter, the way we calculated the area of a circle was to break it up into small segments and add them up in the limit that the size of the segments became infinitesimally small. The same kind of technique works with calculating the area under the graph in Figure 10.8. What we do is divide up that area into many thin rectangles, as shown in Figure 10.9.

If we just added up the areas of all the rectangles, then we'd just get an approximate answer for the area under the graph. To get an exact answer, we need to take the limit of that sum when the width of the rectangles approaches zero. Then it's just a matter of finding an expression for the area of each thin rectangle, an expression for adding up all the areas, and taking the limit of that addition as the width of the rectangles approaches zero. Of course, that's easier said than done. Even for a relatively simple function

Figure 10.8

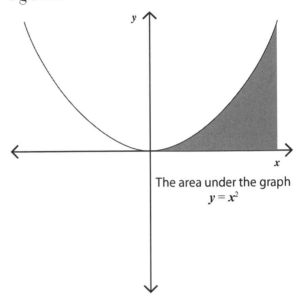

The area under the graph
$y = x^2$

Guidepost Finding the area under a curve using the concept of limits.

Figure 10.9

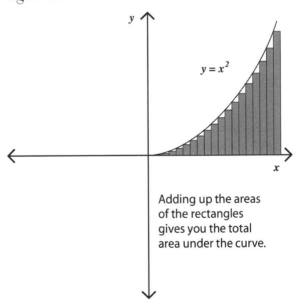

$y = x^2$

Adding up the areas of the rectangles gives you the total area under the curve.

such as $y = x^2$, figuring out that addition is a wee bit too complicated for this book. The result is relatively simple, though. It's just $\frac{x^3}{3}$. To find the area under this graph between any two points x_1 and x_2, you just calculate $\frac{x_2^3}{3} - \frac{x_1^3}{3}$. By the way, the process of adding up infinitesimally small pieces to find an area in two dimensions or a volume in three dimensions is called taking the integral of the function in question. The math symbol that indicates an integral is $\int$. So, when you see an expression like $\int_3^7 x^2 dx$, that represents the area underneath the graph of $y = x^2$ from $x = 3$ to $x = 7$.

If you move to three dimensional shapes and want to calculate a volume, you end up with a double or triple integral, as in $\iint$ or $\iiint$.

Guidepost The definition of an integral.

Aside from examples I'll provide in the Applications section, that's all I'm going to address with respect to calculus. As I said in the intro to this chapter, I just want you to understand the basic concepts behind calculus, and those involve using limits to figure out various otherwise-complicated calculations. When you *do* calculus, you learn all sorts of basic derivatives and integrals and how to calculate many different quantities using those operations. One can even derive equations that contain nothing but first, second, and third derivatives (these are called differential equations) and solve them, resulting in descriptions of quite complicated physical systems. Behind all those computations, though, are the simple ideas presented in this chapter.

Chapter Summary

- A limit is the value one quantity approaches as another quantity approaches a specified value. Limits usually involve one quantity becoming infinitesimally small or infinitesimally large. The basis of calculus involves determining limits in functions that do not vary linearly or are otherwise mathematically complicated.

- The derivative of a function gives you the slope of the function at any particular point.

- The integral of a function gives you the area underneath the graph of the function between any two given points.

- You can use integrals to find the area and volume of both regularly shaped and irregularly shaped objects.

Applications

1. I didn't spend much time in Chapter 9 dealing with the volume of objects, but the idea is basically the same as that for finding the area of something. The difference, of course, is that volume is three-dimensional and area is two-dimensional. In area, you are asking how many square centimeters (or square meters or square inches or whatever) will fit inside a figure. With volume, you are asking how many cubic centimeters (a cube that measures one centimeter on each side) will fit inside a three-dimensional object. Let's see how to figure out the volume of a sphere. Figure 10.10 shows a sphere along with a bunch of cross-sectional disks that make up the sphere.

Figure 10.10

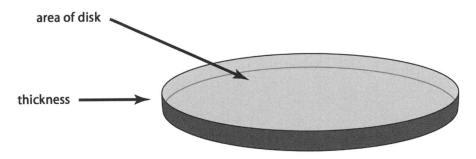

Figure 10.11

area of disk

thickness

Each disk has its own volume. To find the volume of each disk, you would simply multiply the area of the disk by its thickness (see Figure 10.11).

There's a problem, though. Because the surface of the sphere is curved, the thickness of a disk, no matter how thin the disk is, changes gradually. How do we handle something that continually changes? Calculus. You add up the volumes of disks of infinitesimally small thickness by taking the *integral* of the quantity. In fact, since the area of a circle involves a double integral, the volume of the sphere means you have to take a triple integral. Of course, there are other, more clever, ways of doing this triple integral besides adding up the volumes of disks, but the idea is the same. By the way, the result of this triple integral is $\frac{4}{3}\pi r^3$, where r is the radius of the sphere. That's the familiar formula for the volume of a sphere.

2. There are many examples of scientific theories that depend heavily on existing math procedures. One example is Einstein's theory of general relativity, which describes how space-time is curved rather than flat as previously thought. It's not easy to describe the curvature of space-time. Fortunately for Einstein, something in calculus called *differential geometry* existed before he ever developed his theory of general relativity. With lots of confusing symbols, differential geometry explains the geometry of curved surfaces, and allows us to describe the general theory of relativity in mathematical terms. Without it, general relativity would be an interesting idea, but not one that could be addressed with numbers.

Okay, we're at the end of this book on math. There are many, many concepts in math that I haven't covered, but covering all possible concepts isn't the purpose of this book. Primarily I wanted to help you understand the reasoning behind many of the rules of math and, in fact, view mathematics in a different way than you might have before. Hopefully, you have improved your understanding of at least some of the concepts in math, and have gained a perspective that makes you look for understanding rather than memorized rules.

Glossary

addition. The process of combining separate things into one group. Also, something you do with your home when your family gets too large.

additive inverse. What you get when you take the negative (opposite) of a number. When you add the additive inverse of a number to the number, you get 0.

antiparticles. A set of particles that have the opposite charge of regular subatomic particles. Also, particles that do the opposite of what you ask them to do.

area. The amount of two-dimensional space inside a two-dimensional figure.

associative property. A statement that the grouping of terms does not matter in addition and multiplication. There is no associative property for subtraction or division.

Base 2. A number system in which the place values are ones, twos, fours, eights, and other multiple and divisions of the number 2. This is also known as the **binary number system**, and is the language of computers. If you find someone who talks about binary numbers a lot, you just might be talking to a rich computer nerd.

Base 5. A number system in which the place values are ones, fives, twenty fives, and other multiples and divisions of the number 5. No one in his or her right mind uses Base 5 for calculations.

Base 10. A number system in which the place values are ones, tens, hundreds, and all other sorts of multiplications of 10 or divisions by 10. Base 10 is what most of us use when dealing with numbers.

borrow. The process of moving a ten, a hundred, a thousand, and so on, to the next place value column to the right, making subtraction possible. Also something you shouldn't do when dealing with friends and money.

calculus. The mathematics of very small changes. While the basics of calculus are relatively simple, the actual math can get pretty scary looking.

carry. The process of moving a ten, a hundred, a thousand, and so on, to the next place value column to the left. Also, what you do as a parent from the time your kids are born until they leave the house.

circumference. The distance around the edge of a circle.

common denominator. When two or more fractions have different denominators, you can always find equivalent fractions that all have the same denominator, which is known as the common denominator. Also, a very ordinary denominator.

commutative property. A statement that order of terms does not matter in addition and multiplication. There is no commutative property for subtraction or division.

complex number. A number that contains both a real and imaginary part.

cosine. A trigonometric function with values that vary between -1 and 1. In a right triangle, the cosine of an angle is defined as the length of the adjacent side divided by the length of the hypotenuse. Also, something you should never do where a loan is concerned unless you know someone really well.

cross multiplying. A shortcut you can use to solve an equation that has one fraction on each side.

decimal. A method for representing base 10 numbers that contain fractions.

denominator. The generic name for whatever is on bottom in a fraction.

dependent variable. A quantity whose value depends on the value of an independent variable.

derivative. In calculus, the infinitesimal change in one quantity divided by the infinitesimal change in another quantity. The derivative gives you the slope of a curve at any given point.

diameter. The longest straight-line distance across a circle.

distributive property. A property applying to numbers and variables that outlines the proper procedure when multiplying a sum inside parentheses by a quantity outside the parentheses.

division. The reverse of the process of multiplication. Breaking things apart into smaller groups.

equation. A math statement that says whatever is to the left of an equals sign is equal to whatever is to the right of that equals sign. An equation can represent either a true statement or an untrue statement.

equivalent fractions. Fractions that have different numerators and denominators, yet represent the same number.

exponent. A shortcut notation for repeated multiplication of a number by itself.

factor-label method. The process of converting units such as miles per hour to equivalent but different units. You do this by repeatedly multiplying by the number 1, disguised as a fraction involving units.

FOIL. A mnemonic that represents a shortcut to use when multiplying two terms that are each a sum inside a set of parentheses. FOIL represents First, Outside, Inside, Last.

fraction. A part of a whole. Also a representation of the operation of division. Also, how much of what I say to my daughter that actually registers with her.

function. A math relationship in which there is only one value of a dependent variable for each value of an independent variable.

hypotenuse. The longest side of a triangle.

i. A letter that represents the square root of -1.

imaginary number. A number that includes the square root of a negative number, or is multiplied by the square root of a negative number. What math geeks had as young children rather than imaginary friends.

independent variable. A quantity that one can vary independently.

inequality. A math statement that says whatever is to the left of a less-than or greater-than symbol is less-than or greater-than whatever is to the right of that symbol. An inequality can represent either a true statement or an untrue statement.

integers. The set of positive and negative numbers, including 0, that are members of the following group: ...-4, -3, -2, -1, 0, 1, 2, 3, 4, ...

integral. The sum of a number of infinitesimally small quantities. The integral gives you the area underneath a graph between any two points.

irrational number. A number that can be carried out to an infinite number of decimal places without any repeating pattern. Irrational numbers include the square root of 2 and π. Also, a number that can fly off the handle at the slightest provocation.

kinematic equations. A set of equations that describe the relationship between position, speed, and acceleration for cases of constant acceleration.

like terms. Math terms that have identical variables that have identical exponents.

limit. A value one can approach to within an arbitrarily small amount without ever reaching it. When talking about speed limits, however, you can just zoom right through and past that limit if you want.

linear relationship. A math relationship between two variables in which there are no exponents other than 1. When you graph a linear relationship, you get a straight line.

logarithm. When 10 raised to the power of one number equals a second number, the logarithm of the second number is equal to the first number.

multiplication. A shortcut notation for repeated addition. Something rabbits do well.

number line. A line on which you can represent all real numbers, both negative and positive. Number lines are useful for figuring out basic math operations.

numerator. The generic name for whatever is on top in a fraction.

ordered pair. A notation, such as (5, 9), that describes where a point is on a set of vertical and horizontal axes.

parallelogram. A two-dimensional figure that has opposite sides that are parallel and equal in length.

PEMDAS. A mnemonic that helps you remember the proper order of operations in evaluating math expressions.

perimeter. The distance around the edge of any two-dimensional object.

place value. The convention that various written numbers represent the number of ones, tens, hundreds, and so on, contained in a quantity. For example, 15 in base 10 represents one ten and five ones. When using bases other than base 10, the place values change.

point-slope equation. An equation of a line that is of the form $y - y_1 = m(x - x_1)$

Pythagorean theorem. A statement of the relationship between the lengths of the sides and hypotenuse in a right triangle. The sum of the squares of the lengths of the sides is equal to the square of the hypotenuse.

radical. The positive square root of a number or expression. Also, someone rather extreme in his or her political views.

radius. The straight-line distance from the center of a circle to its edge. Also, a bone in your arm.

reciprocal. The reciprocal of a number is 1 divided by that number. In the case of a fraction, you simply reverse the numerator and denominator to find the reciprocal. A number times its reciprocal is equal to 1.

rectangle. A special case of a parallelogram in which all angles are right angles.

remainder. What's left over when you do a division problem without using decimals.

sampling. The process of inferring something about a large population based on a relatively small sample of that population.

scientific notation. A way of representing very large and very small numbers using base 10 exponents. Also, something a scientist might write on a napkin or in the margins of a paper.

sine. A trigonometric function with values that vary between -1 and 1. In a right triangle, the sine of an angle is defined as the length of the opposite side divided by the length of the hypotenuse. Also, something people look for to indicate that they should change their lives.

slope. Often described as the rise divided by the run of a graph, this is more precisely described as the difference in two y values divided by the difference in the corresponding x values.

slope-intercept equation. An equation of a line that is of the form $y = mx + b$

square. A special case of a parallelogram in which all sides are of equal length and all angles are right angles.

square root. If one number multiplied by itself equals a second number, the first number is the square root of the second number.

subtraction. The reverse of the process of addition. You can think of subtraction as adding the opposite of a quantity. Also, what the IRS does to your paycheck.

tangent. A trigonometric function with values that vary between negative infinity and infinity. In a right triangle, the tangent of an angle is defined as the length of the opposite side divided by the length of the adjacent side. A tangent is also a line that is parallel to the slope of a curve at any point. Also, something people get off on when they can't focus their conversation.

transfer problem. A problem that looks on the surface to be completely different from those students have already encountered, but that actually requires concepts that the students have already encountered. Transfer problems are a traditional way to distinguish between students who understand concepts and students who primarily memorize procedures. Also, a problem you can have when switching buses.

triangle. A three-sided, closed, two-dimensional figure.

trigonometry. The mathematics of triangles, angles, and associated functions.

unlike terms. Math terms that do not have identical variables that have identical exponents.

variable. A letter that represents an unknown quantity.

volume. The amount of three-dimensional space inside a three-dimensional object. Also, how loud something is.

word equation. An intermediate step in the translation of a real-world situation into a math equation.

word problems. Math problems that require a translation of a real-world situation into a math equation. Not many people will tell you that word problems are their favorite part of math.

y-intercept. The point at which a graph crosses the y axis.

π. The symbol that represents the circumference of a circle divided by its diameter.

Index

Page numbers in **boldface type** indicate figures.